GW00566555

Business Maths and English

June 2004

Workbook

In this June 2004 first edition

- Introduction to basic maths

- Probability and financial maths

- Writing 'business' English

- Examples of memos, reports and letters

BPP

PROFESSIONAL EDUCATION

First edition June 2004

ISBN 0 7517 1580 8

British Library Cataloguing-in-Publication Data
A catalogue record for this book
is available from the British Library

Published by

BPP Professional Education
Aldine House, Aldine Place
London W12 8AW

www.bpp.com

Printed in Great Britain by W M Print

All our rights reserved. No part of this publication may
be reproduced, stored in a retrieval system or
transmitted, in any form or by any means, electronic,
mechanical, photocopying, recording or otherwise,
without the prior written permission of BPP
Professional Education.

©
BPP Professional Education
2004

Contents

BPP
PROFESSIONAL EDUCATION

Part A: Business Maths

BPP
PROFESSIONAL EDUCATION

chapter 1

The basics

Contents

1 Introduction

This chapter revises the basics of additions, subtraction, multiplication and division. We will also look at the order of calculations and the use of formulae and equations.

2 Basic arithmetic

2.1 Addition

Can you add numbers together in your head or do you automatically reach for your calculator? Normally this reflects a lack of confidence in your mathematical ability. The purpose of this and the following sections is to increase your confidence.

What does the number 5,760,000 represent? Look at it in another way.

1,000,000	100,000	10,000	1,000	100	10	1
5	7	6	0	0	0	0

If you use this type of notation, it makes it easy to add together large numbers. For example, what is 5,760,000 + 12,050,176? Write the numbers out in the new notation and add the columns together starting on the right.

10,000,000	1,000,000	100,000	10,000	1,000	100	10	1
	5	7	6	0	0	0	0
1	2	0	5	0	1	7	6
1	7	8	1	0	1	7	6
		+1					

The answer is 17,810,176. You will notice that the 100,000 column has +1 under it. When adding together the 10,000 column, 6 + 5 = 11. This is 110,000, so we put 1 in the 10,000 column and add 1 to the 100,000 column.

Activity 1.1

Try adding the following numbers together without using a calculator.

(a)   125,125 + 763,579

(b)   1,760,220 + 5,120,763

(c)   12,175,175 + 4,321,000

(d)   125,743,689 + 152,347,986

(e)   146,720 + 220,540 + 325,760

2.2 Subtraction

Subtraction can be carried out in exactly the same way, working in columns from the right but this time subtracting the lower from the upper figure.

For example, what is 17,810,176 – 12,050,176? From the previous section, you should know that the answer is 5,760,000 , but let's prove it.

10,000,000	1,000,000	100,000	10,000	1,000	100	10	1
1	7	8	1	0	1	7	6
1	2	0	5	0	1	7	6
	5	7	6	0	0	0	0
		–1	+10				

Answer: 5,760,000

Did you have problems with the 10,000 column? $1 – 5 = – 4$, but we cannot have a negative number in the middle of a positive one! The answer is to 'borrow' 100,000 from that column. Hence the notation under the 100,000 of '–1' to show a reduction of 100,000 and the '+ 10' under the 10,000 column to show an addition of 100,000. We then have $11 – 5 = 6$.

Activity 1.2

Try the following subtractions, without using a calculator.

(a)   4,760,220 – 2,950,000

(b)   15,765,432 – 4,560,789

(c)   125,125,125 – 74,568,123

If you subtract a larger number from a smaller number, the answer will negative. This is indicated by a minus sign before the number or, more usually in accounting, by putting the number in brackets.

So if we reversed the previous example: 12,050,176 – 17,860,176 is –5,760,000 or (5,760,000).

Remember if you are ever uncertain of your subtraction that your answer added to the number subtracted must always equal the original number. So 5,760,000 + 12,050,176 should equal 17,810,176.

10,000,000	1,000,000	100,000	10,000	1,000	100	10	1
	5	7	6	0	0	0	0
1	2	0	5	0	1	7	6
1	7	8	1	0	1	7	6
		+1					

Answer: 17,810,176

2.3 Multiplication

Multiplication is simply a quick way of adding together the same number many times.

For example, 1,500 × 3 is the same as 1,500 + 1,500 + 1,500. However you can quickly see that the more numbers to be added together, the more cumbersome the addition becomes. Therefore multiplication is used as a short cut.

1,000	100	10	1	
1	5	0	0	
0			3	×
4	5	0	0	
+1				

Answer: 4,500

Remember the following rules.

- 0 × any number = 0
- To multiply by 10, add a zero to the end of a number, eg 5 × 10 = 50
- To multiply by 100, add '00' to the end of the number, eg 5 × 100 = 500, etc.

2.4 Division

Division is another way of finding out which number can be subtracted a number of times. So 4,500 ÷ 3 is another way of asking what number can be subtracted three times from 4,500 without leaving a remainder. In this case, we start with the column on the **left hand side** and remember that 0 divided by anything is still 0.

1,000	100	10	1	
4	5	0	0	
			3	÷
1	5	0	0	
	+10			

Answer: 1,500

Notice that four does not divide exactly by 3. Three divided by 3 is 1, but this leaves 1,000 over. We carry this forward to the 100 column by showing +10 underneath. Fifteen (5 + 10) divided by 3 is then 5.

Activity 1.3

Try these multiplications and divisions, without using a calculator.

(a)   5,321,789 × 12
(b)   14,765,720 × 100
(c)   14,765,720 ÷ 10
(d)   17,625,450 ÷ 50

BPP PROFESSIONAL EDUCATION

2.5 Use in accounting

Basic mathematical calculations are used all the time in accountancy. For example you may be given an annual figure for rent of £24,000 pa. However you need to know the monthly rental figure. Simply divide the annual figure by 12 to get the monthly rental. Here the answer is £24,000 ÷ 12 or £2,000 per month. If you need a quarterly figure (ie the rent for 3 months) you can calculate it in one of two ways.

(a)   £24,000 ÷ 12 × 3 = £6,000
(b)   £24,000 ÷ 4 = £6,000

3 Order of operations

3.1 Brackets

Brackets are used to indicate which parts of a calculation should be done first. In other words, brackets can indicate a **priority**, or an **order** in which calculations should be made. The rule is as follows.

(a)   Do things in brackets before doing things outside them.

(b)   Subject to rule (a), do things in this order.

- Powers and roots
- Multiplications and divisions, working from left to right
- Additions and subtractions, working from left to right

Brackets are used for the sake of clarity. Here are some examples.

(a) $3 + 6 \times 8 = 51$. This is the same as writing $3 + (6 \times 8) = 51$.

(b) $(3 + 6) \times 8 = 72$. The brackets indicate that we wish to multiply the sum of 3 and 6 by 8.

(c) $12 - 4 \div 2 = 10$. This is the same as writing $12 - (4 \div 2) = 10$.

(d) $(12 - 4) \div 2 = 4$. The brackets tell us to do the subtraction first.

A figure outside a bracket may be multiplied by two or more figures inside a bracket, linked by addition or subtraction signs. Here is an example.

$5(6 + 8) = 5 \times (6 + 8) = 5 \times 14 = 70$

The multiplication sign after the 5 can be omitted, as shown here $(5(6 + 8))$, but there is no harm in putting it in $(5 \times (6 + 8))$ if you want to.

Similarly:

$5(8 - 6) = 5(2) = 10$; or $5 \times (8 - 6) = 5 \times 2 = 10$

When two sets of figures linked by addition or subtraction signs within brackets are multiplied together, do the calculations in brackets first. Thus:
$(8 + 4)(7 + 2) = (12)(9) = 108$

3.2 Negative numbers

When a negative number (–p) is **added** to another number (q), the net effect is to **subtract** p from q.

(a) $10 + (-6) = 10 - 6 = 4$ (b) $-10 + (-6) = -10 - 6 = -16$

When a negative number (–p) is **subtracted** from another number (q), the net effect is to **add** p to q.

(a) $12 - (-8) = 12 + 8 = 20$ (b) $-12 - (-8) = -12 + 8 = -4$

When a negative number is **multiplied** or **divided** by another negative number, the result is a **positive** number.

(a) $-8 \times (-4) = +32$ (b) $-18/(-3) = +6$

If there is only **one negative number** in a multiplication or division, the result is **negative**.

(a) $-8 \times 4 = -32$ (b) $3 \times (-2) = -6$ (c) $12/(-4) = ^-3$ (d) $-20/5 = -4$

Activity 1.4

Work out the following.

(a) $(72 - 8) - (-2 + 1)$ (c) $8(2 - 5) - (4 - (-8))$

(b) $\dfrac{88 + 8}{12} + \dfrac{(29 - 11)}{-2}$ (d) $\dfrac{-36}{9 - 3} - \dfrac{84}{3 - 10} - \dfrac{-81}{3}$

3.3 Reciprocals

The **reciprocal** of a number is just 1 divided by that number.

For example, the reciprocal of 2 is 1 divided by 2 = ¹/₂. The reciprocal of 3 is 1 divided by 3 = ¹/₃.

3.4 Extra symbols

We will come across several other mathematical signs in this book but there are five which you should learn **now**.

(a)   > means 'greater than'. So 46 > 29 is true, but 40 > 86 is false.
(b)   ≥ means 'is greater than or equal to'. So 4 ≥ 3 and 4 ≥ 4 are true.
(c)   < means 'is less than'. So 29 < 46 is true, but 86 < 40 is false.
(d)   ≤ means 'is less than or equal to'. So 7 ≤ 8 and 7 ≤ 7 are true.
(e)   ≠ means 'is not equal to'. So we could write 100.004 ≠ 100.

BPP
PROFESSIONAL EDUCATION

4 Formulae and equations

4.1 Formulae

So far all our problems have contained specific numbers. When we want to make a general statement we can use letters eg x + y = z. Here x, y and z stand for numbers and are called **variables**.

The use of variables enables us to state general truths about mathematics.

For example:

- x = x
- x^2 = $x \times x$
- If y = $0.5 \times x$, then x = 2 × y

These will be true **whatever** values x and y have. For example, let x = 2 × y.

- If y = 3, x = 2 × y = 6
- If y = 7, x = 2 × y = 14
- If y = 1, x = 2 × y = 2, and so on for any other choice of a value for y.

We can use **variables** to build up useful **formulae**, we can then put in values for the variables, and get out a value for something we are interested in.

For a business, profit = revenue – costs. Since revenue = selling price × units sold, we can say that

profit = selling price × units sold – costs.

'Selling price × units sold – costs' is a formula for profit.

We can then use single letters to make the formula quicker to write.

Let   p   =   profit
        s   =   selling price
        u   =   units sold
        c   =   cost

Then p = s × u – c.

If we are then told that in a particular month, s = £5, u = 30 and c = £118, we can find out the month's profit.

Profit   =   p = s × u – c = £5 × 30 – £118
         =   £150 – £118 = £32

It is usual when writing formulae to leave out multiplication signs between letters. Thus s × u – c can be written as su – c. We will also write (for example) 2x instead of 2 × x.

4.2 Equations

In the above example, su – c was a formula for profit. If we write p = su – c, we have written an **equation**. It says that one thing (profit, p) is **equal** to another (su – c).

Sometimes, we are given an equation with numbers filled in for all but one of the variables. The problem is then to find the number which should be filled in for the last variable. This is called **solving the equation**.

(a) Returning to p = su – c, we could be told that for a particular month s = £4, u = 60 and c = £208. We would then have the **equation** p = £4 × 60 – £208. We can solve this easily by working out £4 × 60 – £208 = £240 – £208 = £32. Thus p = £32.

(b) On the other hand, we might have been told that in a month when profits were £172, 50 units were sold and the selling price was £7. The thing we have not been told is the month's costs, c. We can work out c by writing out the equation.

$$£172 = £7 \times 50 - c$$
$$£172 = £350 - c$$

Add c to both sides of the equation

$$c + £172 = £350 - c + c$$
$$c + £172 = £350$$

Deduct £172 from both sides of the equation

$$c = £350 - £172$$
$$c = £178$$

4.3 The rule for solving equations

To solve an equation, we need to get it into the following form.

Unknown variable = something with just numbers in it, which we can work out.

The rule is that you can do what you like to one side of an equation, so long as you do the same thing to the other side straightaway. The two sides are equal, and they will stay equal so long as you treat them in the same way.

We saw this in calculating c above. Here are some more examples.

(a)
$450 = 3x + 72$	(initial equation: x unknown)
$450 - 72 = 3x$	(deduct 72 from each side)
$\dfrac{378}{3} = x$	(divide each side by 3)
$126 = x$	(work out the left hand side)

(b)
$3y + 2 = 5y - 7$	(initial equation: y unknown)
$3y + 9 = 5y$	(add 7 to each side)
$9 = 2y$	(subtract 3y from each side)
$4^{1}/_{2} = y$	(divide each side by 2)

BPP
PROFESSIONAL EDUCATION

(c)

$$\frac{3x^2 + x}{4x} = 49 \qquad \text{(initial equation: x unknown)}$$

$(3x + 1)/4 = 49$ (cancel x in the numerator and the denominator of the left hand side: this does not affect the value of the left hand side, so we do not need to change the right hand side)

$3x + 1 = 196$ (multiply each side by 4)

$3x = 195$ (subtract 1 from each side)

$x = 65$ (divide each side by 3)

(d)   Our first example was $p = su - c$. We could change this, so as to give a formula for s.

$p = su - c$

$p + c = su$ (add c to each side)

$\dfrac{p + c}{u} = s$ (divide each side by u)

$s = \dfrac{p + c}{u}$ (swap the sides for ease of reading)

Given values for p, c and u we can now find s. We have rearranged the equation to give s in terms of p, c and u.

In equations, you may come across expressions like $3(x + 4y - 2)$. These can be re-written in separate bits without the brackets, simply by multiplying the number outside the brackets by each item inside them. Thus $3(x + 4y - 2) = 3x + 12y - 6$.

Activity 1.5

(a)   Rearrange $x = (3y - 20)^2$ to get an expression for y in terms of x.

(b)   Rearrange $2(y - 4) - 4(x^2 + 3) = 0$ to get an expression for x in terms of y.

5 Simultaneous equations

Simultaneous equations are two or more equations which are satisfied by the same variable values.

The following two linear equations both involve the unknown values x and y. There are as many equations as there are unknowns and so we can find the values of x and y.

$y = 3x + 16$

$2y = x + 72$

We can solve these equations by manipulation (**algebra**).

    (a)   Returning to the original equations, we have:

$$y = 3x + 16 \qquad\qquad (1)$$
$$2y = x + 72 \qquad\qquad (2)$$

    (b)   Rearranging these, we have:

$$y - 3x = 16 \qquad\qquad (3)$$
$$2y - x = 72 \qquad\qquad (4)$$

    (c)   If we now multiply equation (4) by 3, so that the coefficient for x becomes the same as in equation (3) we get:

$$6y - 3x = 216 \qquad\qquad (5)$$
$$y - 3x = 16 \qquad\qquad (3)$$

    (d)   Subtracting (3) from (5) we get:

$$6y - 3x - y + 3x = 216 - 16$$
$$5y = 200$$
$$y = 40$$

    (e)   Substituting 40 for y in any equation, we can derive a value for x. Thus substituting in equation (4) we get:

$$2(40) - x = 72$$
$$80 - 72 = x$$
$$8 = x$$

    (f)   The solution is y = 40, x = 8.

Activity 1.6

Solve the following simultaneous equations using algebra.

$$5x + 2y = 34$$
$$x + 3y = 25$$

BPP
PROFESSIONAL EDUCATION

chapter 2

Ratios, percentages and use of calculators

Contents

1 Introduction

This chapter looks at the calculation of ratios and percentages, and their relationship to fractions and decimals. We will also look at how to use a scientific calculator to calculate roots and powers.

2 Fractions, decimals, percentages and ratios

Look at the following diagram.

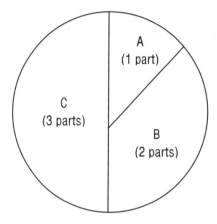

The circle consists of A + B + C ie 1 + 2 + 3 parts, so it is 6 parts in total.

Fractions, decimals, percentages and ratios simply show the relationship of A, B and C to the whole circle or to each other.

2.1 Fractions

A is one part out of a total of 6 parts and is shown as $^1/_6$. Similarly B is $^2/_6$ or $^1/_3$ and C is $^3/_6$ or $^1/_2$. Notice that where the top (numerator) and bottom (denominator) of the fraction are divisible by the same number, we usually reduce the fraction to its simplest form. So with $^2/_6$, both top and bottom can be divided by 2. We do this and reduce the fraction to $^1/_3$. With $^3/_6$, both top and bottom are divisible by 3, reducing the fraction to $^1/_2$.

We can add factors together by finding a common denominator. In our example:

$$A + B + C = \frac{1}{6} + \frac{1}{3} + \frac{1}{2}$$

The common denominator is 6 ($6 \times 1 = 6$; $3 \times 2 = 6$; $2 \times 3 = 6$).

BPP)))
PROFESSIONAL EDUCATION

So: $A + B + C = \dfrac{1}{6} + \dfrac{1 \times 2}{3 \times 2} + \dfrac{1 \times 3}{2 \times 3}$

$= \dfrac{1}{6} + \dfrac{2}{6} + \dfrac{3}{6}$

$= \dfrac{1 + 2 + 3}{6}$

$= \dfrac{6}{6}$

$= 1$

We should expect this as A + B + C is the whole circle and in fractions the whole is 1.

2.2 Decimals

The fraction is another way of saying that the numerator is divided by the denominator. If we actually carry out this division, we arrive at a decimal.

Sometimes the numerator does not divide exactly by the denominator and the final number of the decimal keeps repeating, called **recurring**.

If you divided 1 by 6, you get 0.16666 recurring.

So A as a decimal is 0.1666 recurring, B is 0.3333 recurring and C is 0.5.

2.3 Significant figures and decimal places

Recurring numbers are a problem and one way of overcoming this is to 'round' numbers to the nearest significant figure or decimal place. We do this by discarding all numbers above this. If the first figure to be discarded is equal to or greater than 5, add one to the previous figure. Otherwise the previous figures is unchanged.

Consider 0.16666 recurring. We can restate this in the following ways.

- Correct to three decimal places
  0.167

- Correct to four decimal places
  0.1667

- Correct to three significant figures
  0.167

- Correct to four significant figures
  0.1667

For this example, there is no difference between significant figures and decimal places. However if we were considering 16.1666 recurring there is a difference. For significant figure rounding, we look at the number as a whole, while for decimal place rounding we only round the numbers after the decimal point.

- Correct to three decimal places
  16.167

- Correct to four decimal places
  16.1667

- Correct to three significant figures
  16.2

- Correct to four significant figures
  16.17

Returning to our problem of A, B and C, using rounding correct to two decimal places:

$$A = 0.17$$
$$B = 0.33$$
$$C = 0.50$$

$$A + B + C = 0.17 + 0.33 + 0.50$$
$$= 1.00$$

Again the whole in decimals 1.

2.4 Percentages

To get from decimal to percentage, simply multiply by 100. Using figures correct to two significant figures:

$$A = 0.17 \times 100\%$$
$$= 17\%$$

$$B = 0.33 \times 100\%$$
$$= 33\%$$

$$C = 0.50 \times 100\%$$
$$= 50\%$$

$$A + B + C = 17\% + 33\% + 50\%$$
$$= 100\%$$

The whole is 100%.

2.5 Ratios

Finally a ratio expresses the relationship of A to B, or B to C, or A to B to C. In mathematical notation this is shown as A:B, B:C, A:B:C

Our circle has a total of 6 parts, with A 1 part, B 2 parts and C 3 parts.

Therefore A:B = 1:2; B:C = 2:3 and A:B:C = 1:2:3

3 Use of percentages and ratios in business

Jen's salary is £50,000 per annum. He is to get a 5% increase. What is his new salary?

Increase is 5% of £50,000 $= \dfrac{5}{100} \times 50,000$

$$= \dfrac{5 \times 50,000}{100}$$

$$= \dfrac{250,000}{100}$$

$$= £2,500$$

Therefore Jen's new salary is £50,000 + £2,500 = £52,500.

You may have realised that Jen's new salary is 105% of his old salary. His current salary is 100% and the increase is 5%, so his new salary is 100% + 5% or 105% of his old salary.

New salary $= 105\% \times £50,000$

$$= \dfrac{105}{100} \times £50,000$$

$$= \dfrac{105 \times 50,000}{100}$$

$$= £52,500$$

Activity 2.1

A supplier offering a 17% discount on the list price of washing machines. You are a retailer of washing machines. If the list price is £395 calculate the discounted price.

Sometimes you may be given the discounted figure and need to calculate the starting point ie the 100% figure.

For example, a shop sells a TV set for £175 after giving a cash discount of 5% on the original selling price. What was the original selling price?

The trick is to decide which is the 100% figure. The discount is given an original selling price. So the original selling price is the 100%. The discount is 5% and so the £175 paid is 95% of original selling price.

Original selling price $= \dfrac{175}{95} \times 100$

$$= £184.21$$

Remember that you are dealing with money, so round to two decimal places. In this way you have whole pence!

Activity 2.2

A shop sells fridges for £200, after charging a mark-up of 20% on cost. What is the original cost?

Activity 2.3

In activity 2.2, suppose you were told that the fridges sell for £200, making a gross profit margin of 5%. What is the original cost?

Tutorial note. A gross profit margin of 5% is calculated on selling price. Therefore selling price is the 100% figure.

Ratios can be used to calculate shares of money (eg in a partnership).

Tom and Dick have £24 that they wish to share in the ratio of 2:1. How much will each receive?

The total number of parts is 2 + 1 = 3

The value of one part = £24 ÷ 3 = £8

Tom's share is 2 parts = 2 × £8 = £16

Dick's share is 1 part = 1 × £8 = £8

Check: The total given to Tom and Dick is £16 + £8 = £24.

Activity 2.4

(a)   A, B, C and D want to share £600 in the ratio 6:1:2:3. How much will each receive?

(b)   A, B and C share £1,000 in the ratio: 5:3:2. How much does each receive?

(c)   Bob, Charlie and Dave have £100. They want to share it in the ratio 4:3:3. How much does each receive?

(d)   A, B, C and D have won £12,000 on the lottery. They want to share it in the ratio 2:2:1:1 based on the amounts they put into the syndicate. How much does each receive?

BPP)))
PROFESSIONAL EDUCATION

4 Using calculators

If you have a very basic calculator, you can calculate 20% of 5,000 by using the basic steps: 20 ÷ 199 × 5,000. The number of steps can be reduced by converting 20% to a decimal (0.20) and just doing 0.20 × 5,000. The answer both ways should be 1,000.

However, if your calculator has a % key, why not use that? Simply key in 5,000 × 20 and press the % key. **Warning**: do not press the = key afterwards as this will multiply 5,000 × 1,000!

You may also have a reciprocal key ($^1/_x$). This calculates the reciprocal of any number. The reciprocal of 5 is $^1/_5$ or 0.2. To use the calculator, simply enter 5 and press the $^1/_x$ key, this should immediately give the answer 0.2.

Calculators are also handy for calculating powers and roots. Powers are a number multiplied by itself. So the square of 2 is 2 × 2 = 4 and the mathematical notion is 2^2. The cube of 2 is written 2^3 and is 2 × 2 × 2 = 8. Some calculators have a powers key x^y. If you want to calculate 3^4, press 3, the x^y key and 4. This will calculate 3^4 for you.

Roots go the opposite way to powers, so the square root of 4 is 2. This is shown as $\sqrt{4} = 2$. Most calculators have a square root key (Sqrt). Simply enter the number and press Sqrt. So to calculate $\sqrt{64}$, enter 64 and press Sqrt. This gives the answer 8.

Activity 2.5

Calculate the square roots of the following numbers. You may use a calculator, if necessary.

(a) $\sqrt{16}$

(b) $\sqrt{900}$

(c) $\sqrt{3,025}$

(d) $\sqrt{14,641}$

Calculators can be useful for multi-part calculations by using the memory. Suppose you want to calculate (5 × 7) + (6 × 2) + (27 × 5), using a calculator.

Step 1:   Key in 5 × 7 =, you should get the answer 35. Put this into memory by pressing the M+ key.

Step 2:   Clear the calculator by pressing the CE key (clear last entry).

Step 3:   Key in 6 × 2 =, you should get the answer 12. Again put this into memory by pressing the M+ key.

Step 4:   Again clear the calculator by pressing the CE key.

Step 5:   Key in 27 × 5 =, you should get the answer 135. Put this into memory (M+ key).

Step 6:   Clear calculator by using CE.

Step 7: Recall memory by pressing the MR key. This will give the answer to the problem of 182 (35 + 12 + 135 = 182).

Step 8: Clear the memory by pressing the MC key

Note M+ = add to memory

MS = memory subtotal

MR = memory recall

MC = memory clear

chapter 3

Errors and approximation

Contents

1 Introduction

No matter how hard we try to be accurate, we all make mistakes in calculations at some time. Quite often it is something simple like forgetting to clear the calculator before starting a new computation.

This chapter deals with spotting errors and using approximate figures.

2 Spotting errors

Mental arithmetic is a useful way of spotting errors. If sales are £295 per month, after months 7 total sales should be just below £2,100 (7 × £300). So if the answer is £1,475 there is an error.

Another useful check when multiplying numbers is to check the last digit. £293.64 × 7 is probably beyond most people's mental arithmetic, but we know that 4 × 7 = 28 and so the last digit of the answer should be 8. If it isn't then there is an error. For the record, £293.64 × 7 = £2,055.48.

Another way of checking for an error is whether an answer is reasonable. Try the following activity.

Activity 3.1

(a)   You have calculated Biff's weekly wages as a counter assistant in a fast food shop as £1,089.67. Likely or unlikely?

(b)   Kipper's gross pay for the year to date is £6,211.67 according to your working schedules. It is Month 3 (ie Kipper has received three months' salary). You know that Kipper's annual salary is in the region of £25,000. Is this gross pay to date a likely figure? (*Do not* use a calculator!)

(c)   Molly's salary this month includes a large overtime payment because she has been working in the evenings and at weekends getting ready for the annual audit. If she has done 30 hours of overtime at £15 per hour, and her annual salary is £18,000, does it seem reasonable that her gross pay this month has been calculated as £1,545?

3 Rounding

There are three methods of rounding and these will be illustrated using the figure 18,600.

(a)   **Rounding up**. 18,600 would be expressed as 19,000 to the nearest thousand above.

(b)   **Rounding down**. 18,600 would be expressed as 18,000 to the nearest thousand below.

(c)   **Rounding to the nearest round amount**. 18,600 would be expressed as 19,000 to the nearest thousand. This is the most commonly used method.

In rounding to the **nearest unit**, a value ending in 0.5 is usually rounded up. Thus 3.5 rounded to the nearest unit would be 4.

Rounding can be specified to the **nearest whole unit** (as above), by the **number of decimal places** (3.94712 to 2 decimal places is 3.95), or by the **number of significant figures** (as covered in Chapter 2).

Activity 3.2

(a) What is £482,365.15 to the nearest:

(i)	£1	
(ii)	£100	
(iii)	£1,000	
(iv)	£10,000	

(b) What is 843.668 correct to:

(i)	one decimal place	
(ii)	two decimal places?	

4 Maximum errors

4.1 Absolute errors

Suppose that the population of a country is stated as 40 million. It is quite likely that this figure has been rounded to the nearest million. We could therefore say that the country's population is 40 million ± 500,000 where 40 million is the **estimate** of the population and 500,000 is the **maximum absolute error**.

In general terms an estimate with a maximum absolute error can be expressed as a ± b.

4.2 Relative errors

The error in the population of the country could also be expressed as 40 million ± 1.25%, where 500,000 is 1.25% of 40 million. In this instance the maximum error is a **maximum relative error** and is calculated as

$$\frac{\text{maximum absolute error}}{\text{estimate}} \times 100\%.$$

5 Approximations and errors

If calculations are made using values that have been rounded then the results of such calculations will only be **approximate**. However, provided that we are aware of the maximum errors that can occur, we can still draw conclusions from the results of the calculations.

There are two rules to remember when performing calculations involving rounded or approximate numbers.

(a) **Addition/subtraction**. When two or more rounded or approximate numbers are added or subtracted the **maximum absolute error** in the result equals the sum of the individual maximum absolute errors.

(b) **Multiplication/division**. When two or more rounded or approximate numbers are multiplied or divided, the **approximate maximum relative error** in the result is obtained by adding the individual maximum relative errors.

Example: errors

A chemical producer plans to sell 50,000 litres (to the nearest 1,000 litres) of a particular chemical at a price of £10 (to the nearest pound) per litre.

The cost of materials used to produce the chemicals is expected to be £100,000 but depending on wastage levels this is subject to an error of ± 5%. Labour costs are estimated to be £300,000 ± 10%, depending on overtime working and pay negotiations.

Required

Calculate the maximum absolute error and the maximum relative error in revenue and costs of production.

Solution

	Estimate	Maximum absolute error	Maximum relative error %
Quantity sold	50,000 litres	500 litres*	1
Price	£10	£0.50**	5
Materials	£100,000	£5,000	5
Labour	£300,000	£30,000	10

* This is because 41,500 litres would be rounded up to 42,000 litres but 41,499 litres would be rounded down to 41,000 litres.

** This is because £9.50 would be rounded up to £10 but £9.49 would be rounded down to £9.00.

(a) **Revenue** = quantity sold × price
= (50,000 ± 1%) × (£10 ± 5%)
= (50,000 × £10) ± (1% + 5%)
= £500,000 ± 6%
= £500,000 ± £30,000
∴ Approximate maximum absolute error = £30,000

Approximate maximum relative error = 6%

Note that we need to use relative errors when doing multiplication/division calculations.

(b)   **Costs of production**   = material + labour

$$= (£100,000 \pm £5,000) + (£300,000 \pm £30,000)$$
$$= (£100,000 + £300,000) \pm (£5,000 + £30,000)$$
$$= £400,000 \pm £35,000$$
$$= £400,000 \pm 8.75 \%$$

∴   Maximum absolute error = £35,000

Maximum relative error = 8.75%

Note that we need to use absolute errors when doing addition/subtraction calculations.

Let's see what the actual error would have been.

Maximum revenue   = maximum quantity × maximum price

$$= (50,000 + 1\%) \times (£10 + 5\%)$$
$$= 50,500 \times £10.50$$
$$= £530,250$$

∴ Our approximation of the maximum absolute error was correct to within £(530,250 − 530,000) = £250.

Activity 3.3

The management accountant for Kent Ltd has established the cost of materials for a unit of product T as £10 to the nearest £1.

What are the maximum absolute and the maximum relative errors in the cost?

	Maximum absolute error	Maximum relative error
A	£0.50	10%
B	£0.50	5%
C	£1.00	10%
D	£1.00	5%

chapter 4

Probability and financial maths

Contents

1 Introduction

This chapter acts as an introduction to probability theory. The term probability is simply the mathematical term used when there is uncertainty.

You have seen, and probably been approached by, market researchers in the High Street. They are asking a 'sample' of the population for their views. The results are then analysed and conclusions reached on the grounds of probability ie that the views of the sample reflect the views of the whole. Later in this chapter, we will look at financial maths with an introduction to interest and discounting.

2 The concept of probability

Probability is a measure of likelihood and can be stated as a percentage, a ratio, or more usually as a number from 0 to 1.

Consider the following.

- Probability = 0 = impossibility
- Probability = 1 = certainty
- Probability = ½ = a 50% chance of something happening
- Probability = ¼ = a 1 in 4 chance of something happening

In statistics, **probabilities** are more commonly expressed as **proportions** than as **percentages**. Consider the following possible outcomes.

Possible outcome	Probability as a percentage	Probability as a proportion
A	15.0%	0.150
B	20.0%	0.200
C	32.5%	0.325
D	7.5%	0.075
E	12.5%	0.125
F	12.5%	0.125
	100.0%	1.000

It is useful to consider how probability can be quantified. A businessman might estimate that if the selling price of a product is raised by 20p, there would be a 90% probability that demand would fall by 30%, but how would he have reached his estimate of 90% probability?

There are several ways of assessing probabilities.

- They may be measurable with **mathematical certainty**.

  - If a coin is tossed, there is a 0.5 probability that it will come down heads, and a 0.5 probability that it will come down tails.

  - If a die is thrown, there is a one-sixth probability that a 6 will turn up.

- They may be measurable from an analysis of **past experience**.

- Probabilities can be estimated from **research** or **surveys**.

It is important to note that probability is a measure of the likelihood of an event happening in the long run, or over a large number of times.

3 The laws of probability

It is the year 2020 and examiners are extinct. A mighty but completely fair computer churns out examinations that are equally likely to be easy or difficult. There is no link between the number of questions on each paper, which is arrived at on a fair basis by the computer, and the standard of the paper. You are about to take five examinations.

3.1 Simple probability

It is vital that the first examination is easy as it covers a subject which you have tried, but unfortunately failed, to understand. What is the probability that it will be an easy examination?

Obviously (let us hope), the probability of an easy paper is $1/2$ (or 50% or 0.5). This reveals a very important principle (which holds if each result is equally likely).

Formula to learn

Probability of achieving the desired result

$$= \frac{\text{Number of ways of achieving desired result}}{\text{Total number of possible outcomes}}$$

Let us apply the principle to our example.

Total number of possible outcomes = 'easy' or 'difficult'	= 2
Total number of ways of achieving the desired result (which is 'easy')	= 1
The probability of an easy examination, or P(easy examination)	= $1/2$

Example: simple probability

Suppose that a coin is tossed in the air. What is the probability that it will come down heads?

Solution

$$P(\text{heads}) = \frac{\text{Number of ways of achieving desired result (heads)}}{\text{Total number of possible outcomes (heads or tails)}}$$

$$= \quad 1/2 \text{ or } 50\% \text{ or } 0.5.$$

3.2 Complementary outcomes

You are desperate to pass more of the examinations than your sworn enemy but, unlike you, he is more likely to pass the first examination if it is difficult. (He is very strange!!) What is the probability of the first examination being more suited to your enemy's requirements?

We know that the probability of certainty is one. The certainty in this scenario is that the examination will be easy or difficult.

P(easy or difficult examination)	=	1
From above, P(easy examination)	=	½
P(not easy examination)	=	P(difficult examination)
	=	1 – P(easy examination)
	=	1 – ½
	=	½

Formula to learn

$$P(\overline{A}) = 1 - P(A), \text{ where } \overline{A} \text{ is 'not A'.}$$

Example: complementary outcomes

If there is a 25 per cent chance of the Rainbow Party winning the next general election, use the law of complementary events to calculate the probability of the Rainbow Party *not* winning the next election.

Solution

P(winning)	=	25% = ¼
P(not winning)	=	1 – P(winning) = 1 – ¼ = ¾

3.3 The simple addition or OR law

The time pressure in the second examination is enormous. The computer will produce a paper which will have between five and nine questions. You know that, easy or difficult, the examination must have six questions at the most for you to have any hope of passing it.

What is the probability of the computer producing an examination with six or fewer questions? In other words, what is the probability of an examination with five *or* six questions?

Don't panic. Let us start by using the basic principle.

P(5 questions) $\quad=\quad$ $\dfrac{\text{Total number of ways of achieving a five question examination}}{\text{Total number of possible outcomes (= 5,6,7,8 or 9 questions)}}$

$\quad=\quad {}^1/_5$

Likewise P(6 questions) $\quad=\quad {}^1/_5$

Either five questions or six questions would be acceptable, so the probability of you passing the examination must be greater than if just five questions or just six questions (but not both) were acceptable. We therefore add the two probabilities together so that the probability of passing the examination has increased.

So P(5 or 6 questions) $\quad=\quad$ P(5 questions) + P(6 questions)

$\quad=\quad {}^1/_5 + {}^1/_5 = {}^2/_5$

Assessment formula

The **simple addition law** or **OR law** is:

P(A or B) = P(A) + P(B)

where A and B are **mutually exclusive outcomes**, which means that the occurrence of one of the outcomes excludes the possibility of any of the others happening.

In the example the outcomes are **mutually exclusive** because it is impossible to have five questions *and* six questions in the same examination.

Example: mutually exclusive outcomes

The delivery of an item of raw material from a supplier may take up to six weeks from the time the order is placed. The probabilities of various delivery times are as follows.

Delivery time	Probability
≤ 1 week	0.10
> 1, ≤ 2 weeks	0.25
> 2, ≤ 3 weeks	0.20
> 3, ≤ 4 weeks	0.20
> 4, ≤ 5 weeks	0.15
> 5, ≤ 6 weeks	0.10
	1.00

Required

Calculate the probability that a delivery will take the following times.

(a)   Two weeks or less
(b)   More than three weeks

Solution

(a)   P ($\leq$ 1 or > 1, $\leq$ 2 weeks)   =   P ($\leq$ 1 week) + P (>1, $\leq$ 2 weeks)

                                                    =   0.10 + 0.25

                                                    =   0.35

(b)   P (> 3, $\leq$ 6 weeks)   =   P (> 3, $\leq$ 4 weeks) + P (> 4, $\leq$ 5 weeks) + P (> 5, $\leq$ 6 weeks)

                                                    =   0.20 + 0.15 + 0.10

                                                    =   0.45

3.4 The simple multiplication or AND law

You still have three examinations to sit: astrophysics, geography of the moon and computer art. Stupidly, you forgot to revise for the astrophysics examination, which will have between 15 and 20 questions. You think that you may scrape through this paper if it is easy *and* if there are only 15 questions.

What is the probability that the paper the computer produces will exactly match your needs? Do not forget that there is no link between the standard of the examination and the number of questions.

The best way to approach this question is diagrammatically, showing all the possible outcomes.

				Number of questions		
	15	*16*	*17*	*18*	*19*	*20*
Type of paper						
Easy (E)	E and 15*	E and 16	E and 17	E and 18	E and 19	E and 20
Difficult (D)	D and 15	D and 16	D and 17	D and 18	D and 19	D and 20

The diagram shows us that, of the twelve possible outcomes, there is only one 'desired result' (which is asterisked). We can therefore calculate the probability as follows.

P(easy paper *and* 15 questions) = $^1/_{12}$.

The answer can be found more easily as follows.

P(easy paper *and* 15 questions) = P(easy paper) $\times$ P(15 questions) = $^1/_2 \times {}^1/_6 = {}^1/_{12}$.

Assessment formula

The **simple multiplication law** or **AND law** is: P(A and B) = P(A) P(B)

where A and B are **independent** events, which means that the occurrence of one event in no way affects the outcome of the other events.

The number of questions has no effect on, nor is it affected by whether it is an easy or difficult paper.

Example: independent events

A die is thrown and a coin is tossed simultaneously. What is the probability of throwing a 5 and getting heads on the coin?

Solution

The probability of throwing a 5 on a die is $^1/_6$
The probability of a tossed coin coming up heads is ½
The probability of throwing a 5 and getting heads on a coin is $½ \times ^1/_6 = ^1/_{12}$

3.5 The general rule of addition

The three examinations you still have to sit are placed face down in a line in front of you at the final examination sitting. There is an easy astrophysics paper, a difficult geography of the moon paper and a difficult computer art paper. Without turning over any of the papers you are told to choose one of them. What is the probability that the first paper that you select is difficult or is the geography of the moon paper?

Let us think about this carefully.

There are two difficult papers, so P(difficult) = $^2/_3$

There is one geography of the moon paper, so P(geography of the moon) = $^1/_3$

If we use the OR law and add the two probabilities then we will have double counted the difficult geography of the moon paper. It is included in the set of difficult papers and in the set of geography of the moon papers. In other words, we are *not* faced with mutually exclusive outcomes because the occurrence of a geography of the moon paper does not exclude the possibility of the occurrence of a difficult paper. We therefore need to take account of this double counting.

P(difficult paper or geography of the moon paper) = P(difficult paper) + P(geography of the moon paper) – P(difficult paper and geography of the moon paper).

Using the AND law, P(difficult paper or geography of the moon paper) = $^2/_3 + ^1/_3 - (^1/_3) = ^2/_3$.

Assessment formula

The **general rule of addition** is: P(A or B) = P(A) + P(B) – P(A and B)

where the word 'or' is used in an inclusive sense: either A or B or both. A and B are therefore *not* mutually exclusive.

Since it is *not* impossible to have an examination which is difficult *and* about the geography of the moon, these two events are not mutually exclusive.

Activity 4.1

If one card is drawn from a normal pack of 52 playing cards, what is the probability of getting an ace or a spade?

Probability

Ace	*Spade*	*Ace of spades*	*Ace or spade*

3.6 The general rule of multiplication

Computer art is your last examination. Understandably you are very tired and you are uncertain whether you will be able to stay awake. You believe that there is a 70% chance of your falling asleep if it becomes too hot and stuffy in the examination hall. It is well known that the air conditioning system serving the examination hall was installed in the last millennium and is therefore extremely unreliable. There is a 1 in 4 chance of it breaking down during the examination, thereby causing the temperature in the hall to rise. What is the likelihood that you will drop off?

The scenario above has led us to face what is known as **conditional probability**. We can rephrase the information provided as 'the probability that you will fall asleep, given that it is too hot and stuffy, is equal to 70%' and we can write this as follows.

P(fall asleep/too hot and stuffy) = 70%.

Whether you fall asleep is **conditional** upon whether the hall becomes too hot and stuffy. The events are not, therefore, independent and so we cannot use the simple multiplication law. So:

P(it becomes too hot and stuffy and you fall asleep)

=   P(too hot and stuffy) × P(fall asleep/too hot and stuffy)

=   25% × 70% = 0.25 × 0.7 = 0.175 = $17\frac{1}{2}$%

Assessment formula

The **general rule of multiplication** is: P(A and B) =P(A) × P(B/A) =P(B) × P(A/B)

where A and B are **dependent** (ie not independent) events, the occurrence of the second event being dependent upon the occurrence of the first.

When A and B are independent events, then P(B/A) = P(B) since, by definition, the occurrence of B (and therefore P(B)) does not depend upon the occurrence of A. Similarly P(A/B) = P(A).

Example: conditional probability

The board of directors of Shuttem Ltd has warned that there is a 60% probability that a factory will be closed down unless its workforce improves its productivity. The factory's manager has estimated that the probability of success in agreeing a productivity deal with the workforce is only 30%.

Required

Determine the likelihood that the factory will be closed.

Solution

If outcome A is the shutdown of the factory and outcome B is the failure to improve productivity:

$$P \text{ (A and B)} = P(B) \times P(A/B)$$
$$= 0.7 \times 0.6$$
$$= 0.42$$

Another method of dealing with some conditional probabilities is by using contingency tables. Their use is best explained by an example.

Example: contingency tables

A cosmetics company has developed a new anti-dandruff shampoo which is being tested on volunteers. Seventy percent of the volunteers have used the shampoo whereas others have used a normal shampoo, believing it to be the new anti-dandruff shampoo. Two sevenths of those using the new shampoo showed no improvement whereas one third of those using the normal shampoo had less dandruff.

Required

A volunteer shows no improvement. What is the probability that he used the normal shampoo?

Solution

The problem is solved by drawing a contingency table, showing 'improvement' and 'no improvement', volunteers using normal shampoo and volunteers using the new shampoo.

Let us suppose that there were 1,000 volunteers (we could use any number). We could depict the results of the test on the 1,000 volunteers as follows.

	New shampoo	Normal shampoo	Total
Improvement	***500	****100	600
No improvement	**200	200	400
	*700	***300	1,000

* 70% × 1,000   ** $^2/_7$ × 700

*** Balancing figure   **** $^1/_3$ × 300

We can now calculate P(used normal shampoo/showed no improvement)

P(shows no improvement) = 400/1,000

P(used normal shampoo/shows no improvement) = 200/400 = ½

Other probabilities are just as easy to calculate.

P(shows improvement/used new shampoo) = 500/700 = $^5/_7$

P(used new shampoo/shows improvement) = 500/600 = $^5/_6$

Activity 4.2

The independent probabilities that the three sections of a management accounting department will encounter one computer error in a week are respectively 0.1, 0.2 and 0.3. There is never more than one computer error encountered by any one section in a week. Calculate the probability that there will be the following number of errors encountered by the management accounting department next week.

(a) At least one computer error
(b) One and only one computer error

Activity 4.3

In a student survey, 60% of the students are male and 75% are CIMA candidates. The probability that a student chosen at random is either female or a CIMA candidate is:

    A 0.85   B 0.30   C 0.40   D 1.00

4 Probability distributions

If we convert the frequencies in the following frequency distribution table into proportions, we get a **probability distribution**.

Marks out of 10 (statistics test)	Number of students (frequency distribution)	Proportion or probability (probability distribution)
0	0	0.00
1	0	0.00
2	1	0.02*
3	2	0.04
4	4	0.08
5	10	0.20
6	15	0.30
7	10	0.20
8	6	0.12
9	2	0.04
10	0	0.00
	50	1.00

* $\frac{1}{50} = 0.02$

A **probability distribution** is an analysis of the proportion of times each particular value occurs in a set of items.

A graph of the probability distribution would be the same as the graph of the frequency distribution, but with the **vertical axis marked in proportions** rather than in numbers.

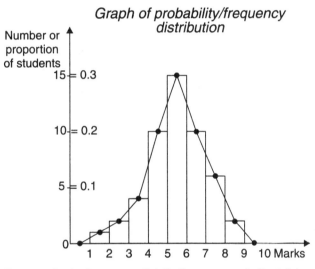

Graph of probability/frequency distribution

(a)   The area under the curve in the frequency distribution represents the total number of students whose marks have been recorded, 50 people.

(b)   **The area under the curve in a probability distribution is 100%, or 1** (the total of all the probabilities).

5 The normal distribution

The normal distribution is an important probability distribution which is often applied to **continuous variables**. In other words, in calculating P(x), x can be any value, and does not have to be a whole number.

The normal distribution can also apply to **discrete variables** which can take **many possible values**. For example, the volume of sales, in units, of a product might be any whole number in the range 100 – 5,000 units. There are so many possibilities within this range that the variable is for all practical purposes **continuous**.

The normal distribution can be drawn as a graph, and it would be a **bell-shaped curve**.

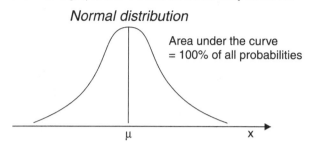

Normal distribution

Area under the curve
= 100% of all probabilities

μ   x

Properties of the normal distribution are as follows.

- It is symmetrical.
- The mean of the distribution is known as μ (pronounced mew).
- The area to the left of μ is the mirror image of the area to the right of μ.
- The area under the curve totals exactly 1.

The normal distribution is important because in the practical application of statistics, it has been found that **many probability distributions are close enough to a normal distribution** to be treated as one without any significant loss of accuracy.

6 The standard deviation and the normal distribution

6.1 Standard deviation

For any normal distribution, the **dispersion** around the mean (μ) of the frequency of occurrences can be measured exactly in terms of the **standard deviation (σ)**.

The entire frequency curve represents all the possible outcomes and their frequencies of occurrence. Since the normal curve is **symmetrical, 50% of occurrences have a value greater than the mean value** (μ), and **50% of occurrences have a value less than the mean value** (μ).

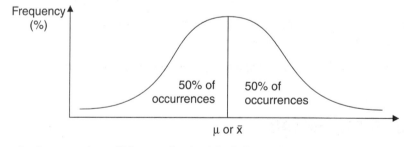

Frequency (%)

50% of occurrences   50% of occurrences

μ or x̄

About 68% of frequencies have a value within one standard deviation either side of the mean. Thus if a normal distribution has a **mean of 80** and a **standard deviation of 3**, 68% (2 × 34%) of the total frequencies would occur

BPP PROFESSIONAL EDUCATION

within the range ± one standard deviation from the mean. Since the curve is symmetrical, 34% of the values must fall in the range 77 – 80 and 34% in the range 80 – 83.

ie mean ± one standard deviation (=3)

=   80 ± 3

=   80 + 3 = 83

or   80 – 3 = 77

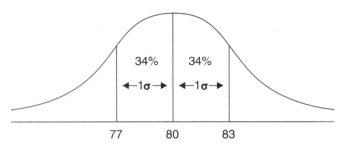

95% of the frequencies in a normal distribution occur in the range ± 1.96 standard deviations from the mean.

In our example, when μ = 80, and σ = 3, 95% of the frequencies in the distribution would occur in the range

mean ± 1.96 standard deviations

        80 ± 1.96 (3)

=   80 ± 5.88 (the range 74.12 to 85.88)

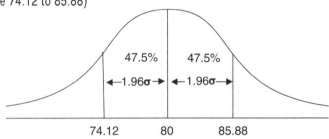

47½% would be in the range 74.12 to 80 and 47½% would be in the range 80 to 85.88.

99% of the frequencies occur in the range ± 2.58 standard deviations from the mean.

In our example, 99% of frequencies in a normal distribution with μ = 80 and σ = 3 would lie in the range

        mean ± 2.58 standard deviations

        80 ± 2.58 (3)

=   80 ± 7.74

=   72.26 to 87.74.

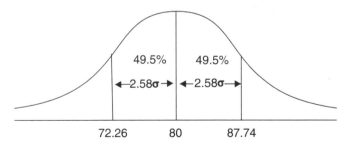

49½% would be in the range 72.26 – 80 and 49½% would be in the range 80 – 87.74

Assessment focus point

x% of the frequencies in a normal distribution occur in the range ± y standard deviations from the mean.

You will save yourself time in an assessment if you learn the following by heart.

- 68% of frequencies occur in the range mean ± 1 standard deviation
- 95% of frequencies occur in the range mean ± 1.96 standard deviations
- 99% of frequencies occur in the range mean ± 2.58 standard deviations

6.2 Normal distribution tables

Although there is an infinite number of normal distributions, depending on values of the mean μ and the standard deviation σ, **the relative dispersion of frequencies around the mean, measured as proportions of the total population, is exactly the same for all normal distributions**. In other words, whatever the normal distribution, 47.5% of outcomes will always be in the range between the mean and 1.96 standard deviations below the mean, 49.5% of outcomes will always be in the range between the mean and 2.58 standard deviations below the mean and so on.

A normal distribution table, shown at the end of this Study Text, gives the proportion of the total between the mean and a point above or below the mean for any multiple of the standard deviation.

Assessment formula

Distances above or below the mean are expressed in numbers of **standard deviations, z.**

$$z = \frac{x - \mu}{\sigma}$$

where
- z = the number of standard deviations above or below the mean (z score)
- x = the value of the variable under consideration
- μ = the mean
- σ = the standard deviation.

Example: normal distribution tables

Calculate the following z scores and identify the corresponding proportions using normal distribution tables.

(a) x = 100, μ = 200, σ = 50
(b) x = 1,000, μ = 1,200, σ = 200
(c) x = 25, μ = 30, σ = 6

BPP PROFESSIONAL EDUCATION

Solution

(a) $z = \dfrac{x - \mu}{\sigma}$

$= \dfrac{100 - 200}{50}$

$= 2$

A z score of 2 corresponds to a proportion of 0.4772 or 47.72%.

(b) $z = \dfrac{x - \mu}{\sigma}$

$= \dfrac{1,000 - 1,200}{200}$

$= 1$

A z score of 1 corresponds to a proportion of 0.3413 or 34.13%.

(c) $z = \dfrac{x - \mu}{\sigma}$

$= \dfrac{25 - 30}{6}$

$= 0.8333$

0.8333 corresponds to a proportion of 0.2967 or 29.67%

If a z score of 1.96 is calculated, what does this mean?

1.96 corresponds to an area of 0.4750 or 47.5%

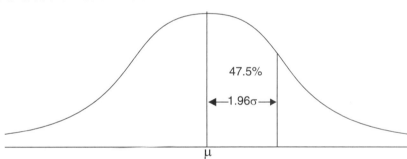

Since the normal distribution is symmetrical 1.96σ below the mean will also correspond to an area of 47.5%.

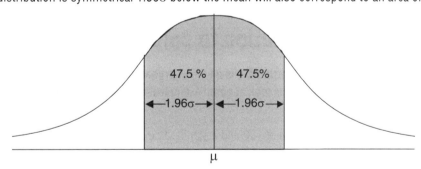

The total shaded area = 47.5% × 2 = 95%

95% of the area under a probability curve therefore lies between mean, μ and 1.96σ above and below the mean. Do you recognise this figure?

We said that 95% of the frequencies in a normal distribution lie in the range ± 1.96 standard deviations from the mean but we did not say what this figure was based on. It was of course based on the corresponding value in the normal distribution tables (when z = 1.96) as shown in the paragraph above.

We also said that 99% of the frequencies occur in the range ± 2.58 standard deviation from the mean.

Why did we say that?

Well, a z score of 2.58 corresponds to an area of 0.4949 (or 49.5%). Remember, the normal distribution is symmetrical.

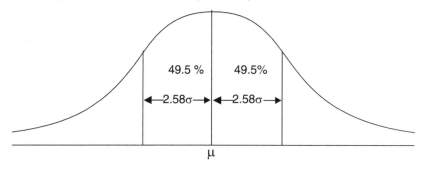

49.5% × 2 = 99%

If   mean, μ + 2.58σ   =   49.5% and
     mean, μ – 2.58σ   =   49.5%
     Range = mean ± 2.58σ   =   99.0%

Therefore, 99% of frequencies occur in the range mean (μ) ± 2.58 standard deviations (σ), as proved by using normal distribution tables.

Activity 4.4

Prove that approximately 68% of frequencies have a value within one standard deviation either side of the mean, μ.

7 Using the normal distribution to calculate probabilities

We have already mentioned that the normal distribution is a type of **probability distribution**. The normal distribution can therefore be used to calculate probabilities. Let's look at some examples to demonstrate how the normal distribution can be used to calculate probabilities.

A frequency distribution is normal, with a mean of 100 and a standard deviation of 10.

BPP
PROFESSIONAL EDUCATION

Required

Calculate the proportion of the total frequencies which will be:

(a)   above 80
(b)   above 90
(c)   above 100
(d)   above 115
(e)   below 85
(f)   below 95
(g)   below 108
(h)   in the range 80 - 110
(i)   in the range 90 - 95

Example: using the normal distribution to calculate the proportion of frequencies above a certain value

If the value (x) is below the mean (μ), the total proportion is **0.5 plus proportion between the value and the mean (area (a))**.

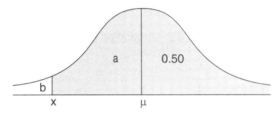

(a)   Using the information above, the proportion of the total frequencies which will be above 80 is calculated as follows.

$$\frac{80 - 100}{10} = 2 \text{ standard deviations } \textbf{below} \text{ the mean.}$$

From the tables, where z = 2 the proportion is 0.4772.

The proportion of frequencies above 80 is 0.5 + 0.4772 = 0.9772.

(b)   Using the information above, the proportion of the total frequencies which will be above 90 is calculated as follows.

$$\frac{90 - 100}{10} = 1 \text{ standard deviation } \textbf{below} \text{ the mean.}$$

From the tables, when z = 1, the proportion is 0.3413.

The proportion of frequencies above 90 is 0.5 + 0.3413 = 0.8413.

(c)   100 is the mean. The proportion above this is 0.5. (The normal curve is symmetrical and 50% of occurrences have a value greater than the mean, and 50% of occurrences have a value less than the mean.)

If the value is above the mean, the proportion (b) **is 0.5 – proportion between the value and the mean (area (a))**.

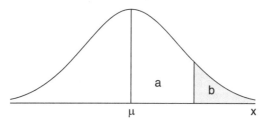

(d)   Using the information in paragraph 4.2, the proportion of the total frequencies which will be above 115 is calculated as follows.

$$\frac{115-100}{10} = 1.5 \text{ standard deviations } \textbf{above} \text{ the mean.}$$

From the tables, where z = 1.5, the proportion is 0.4332.
The proportion of frequencies above 115 is therefore 0.5 – 0.4332 = 0.0668.

Example: using the normal distribution to calculate the proportion of frequencies below a certain value

If the value is below the mean, the proportion (b) is 0.5 – proportion between the value and the mean (area (a)).

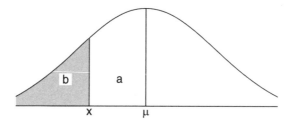

(e)   The proportion of the total frequencies which will be below 85 is calculated as follows.
$$\frac{85-100}{10} = 1.5 \text{ standard deviations } \textbf{below} \text{ the mean.}$$

The proportion of frequencies below 85 is therefore the same as the proportion above 115, 0.0668.

(f)   The proportion of the total frequencies which will be below 95 is calculated as follows.
$$\frac{95-100}{10} = 0.5 \text{ standard deviations } \textbf{below} \text{ the mean.}$$

When z = 0.5, the proportion from the tables is 0.1915. The proportion of frequencies below 95 is therefore 0.5 – 0.1915 = 0.3085.

If the value is **above** the mean, the proportion required (b) is **0.5 plus the proportion between the value and the mean (area (a))**.

BPP)))
PROFESSIONAL EDUCATION

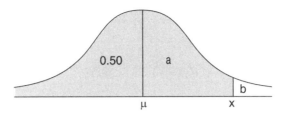

(g)   The proportion of the total frequencies which will be below 108 is calculated as follows.

$$\frac{108 - 100}{10} = 0.8 \text{ standard deviations \textbf{above} the mean.}$$

From the tables for z = 0.8 the proportion is 0.2881.

The proportion of frequencies below 108 is 0.5 + 0.2881 = 0.7881.

Example: using the normal distribution to calculate the proportion of frequencies within a certain range

(h)   The proportion of the total frequencies which will be in the range 80-110 is calculated as follows. The range 80 to 110 may be divided into two parts:

(i)   80 to 100 (the mean);
(ii)   100 to 110.

The proportion in the range 80 to 100 is (2 standard deviations) 0.4772

The proportion in the range 100 to 110 is (1 standard deviation) 0.3413

The proportion in the total range 80 to 110 is 0.4772 + 0.3413 = 0.8185.

(i)   The range 90 to 95 may be analysed as:

(i)   the proportion above 90 and below the mean
(ii)   minus the proportion above 95 and below the mean

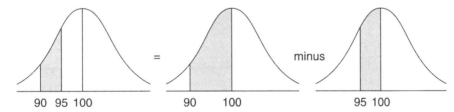

Proportion above 90 and below the mean (1 standard deviation)	0.3413
Proportion above 95 and below the mean (0.5 standard deviations)	0.1915
Proportion between 90 and 95	0.1498

Activity 4.5

The salaries of employees in an industry are normally distributed, with a mean of £14,000 and a standard deviation of £2,700.

Required

(a)   Calculate the proportion of employees who earn less than £12,000.
(b)   Calculate the proportion of employees who earn between £11,000 and £19,000.

Note that **the normal distribution is, in fact, a way of calculating probabilities**.

Activity 4.6

The distribution of sales is normal, with a mean of 1,500 items per week, and a variance of 500 items. The probability that sales are less than 1,300 items in any one week is (delete as appropriate):

15.54%	65.54%
84.46%	34.46%

Activity 4.7

Use the information in Question 4.6 to answer this question.

There is a probability of 30.85% that sales will be above how many items per week?

A   1,550
B   1,650
C   1,750
D   1,850

8 Simple interest

- **Interest** is the amount of money which an investment earns over time.

- **Simple interest** is interest which is earned in equal amounts every year (or month) and which is a given proportion of the original investment (the principal).

If a sum of money is invested for a period of time, then the amount of simple interest which accrues is equal to the number of periods × the interest rate × the amount invested. We can write this as a formula.

Formula to learn

The formula for **simple interest** is as follows.

S = X + nrX

where X = the original sum invested
       r = the interest rate (expressed as a proportion, so 10% = 0.1)
       n = the number of periods (normally years)
       S = the sum invested after n periods, consisting of the original capital (X) plus interest earned.

Example: simple interest

How much will an investor have after five years if he invests £1,000 at 10% simple interest per annum?

Solution

Using the formula S = X + nrX

where X = £1,000
       r = 10%
       n = 5

∴ S = £1,000 + (5 × 0.1 × £1,000) = £1,500

If , for example, the sum of money is invested for 3 months and the interest rate is a rate per annum, then $n = \frac{3}{12} = \frac{1}{4}$. If the investment period is 197 days and the rate is an annual rate, then $n = \frac{197}{365}$.

9 Compound interest

9.1 Compounding

Interest is normally calculated by means of **compounding**.

If a sum of money, the principal, is invested at a fixed rate of interest such that the interest is added to the principal and no withdrawals are made, then the amount invested will grow by an increasing number of pounds in each successive time period, because **interest earned in earlier periods will itself earn interest in later periods**.

Example: compound interest

Suppose that £2,000 is invested at 10% interest. After one year, the original principal plus interest will amount to £2,200.

	£
Original investment	2,000
Interest in the first year (10%)	200
Total investment at the end of one year	2,200

(a)   After two years the total investment will be £2,420.

	£
Investment at end of one year	2,200
Interest in the second year (10%)	220
Total investment at the end of two years	2,420

The second year interest of £220 represents 10% of the original investment, and 10% of the interest earned in the first year.

(b)   Similarly, after three years, the total investment will be £2,662.

	£
Investment at the end of two years	2,420
Interest in the third year (10%)	242
Total investment at the end of three years	2,662

Instead of performing the calculations in Paragraph 2.2, we could have used the following formula.

Assessment formula

The basic formula for **compound interest** is $S = X(1 + r)^n$

where X =   the original sum invested
r =   the interest rate, expressed as a proportion (so 5% = 0.05)
n =   the number of periods
S =   the sum invested after n periods

Using the formula for compound interest, $S = X(1 + r)^n$

where X = £2,000
r = 10% = 0.1
n = 3
S = £2,000 × 1.10^3
= £2,000 × 1.331
= £2,662.

The interest earned over three years is £662, which is the same answer that was calculated in the example above.

Activity 4.8

Simon invests £5,000 now. To what value would this sum have grown after the following periods using the given interest rates? State your answer to two decimal places.

Value now	Investment period	Interest rate	Final value
£	Years	%	£
5,000	3	20	
5,000	4	15	
5,000	3	6	

Activity 4.9

At what annual rate of compound interest will £2,000 grow to £2,721 after four years?

    A 7%   B 8%   C 9%   D 10%

9.2 Inflation

The same compounding formula can be used to **predict future prices** after allowing for **inflation**. For example, if we wish to predict the salary of an employee in five years time, given that he earns £8,000 now and wage inflation is expected to be 10% per annum, the compound interest formula would be applied as follows.

$$S = X(1 + r)^n$$
$$= £8,000 \times 1.10^5$$
$$= £12,884.08$$

say,   £12,900.

9.3 Withdrawals of capital or interest

If an investor takes money out of an investment, it will cease to earn interest. Thus, if an investor puts £3,000 into a bank deposit account which pays interest at 8% per annum, and makes no withdrawals except at the end of year 2, when he takes out £1,000, what would be the balance in his account after four years?

BPP PROFESSIONAL EDUCATION

	£
Original investment	3,000.00
Interest in year 1 (8%)	240.00
Investment at end of year 1	3,240.00
Interest in year 2 (8%)	259.20
Investment at end of year 2	3,499.20
Less withdrawal	1,000.00
Net investment at start of year 3	2,499.20
Interest in year 3 (8%)	199.94
Investment at end of year 3	2,699.14
Interest in year 4 (8%)	215.93
Investment at end of year 4	2,915.07

A quicker approach would be as follows.

	£
£3,000 invested for 2 years at 8% would increase in value to £3,000 $\times$ 1.08^2 =	3,499.20
Less withdrawal	1,000.00
	2,499.20

£2,499.20 invested for a further two years at 8% would increase in value to

£2,499.20 $\times$ 1.08^2 = £2,915.07

10 The concept of discounting

10.1 The basic principles of discounting

The **basic principle of compounding** is that if we invest £X now for n years at r% interest per annum, we should obtain £X $(1 + r)^n$ in n years time.

Thus if we invest £10,000 now for four years at 10% interest per annum, we will have a total investment worth £10,000 $\times$ 1.10^4 = £14,641 at the end of four years (that is, at year 4 if it is now year 0).

The basic principle of **discounting** is that if we wish to have £V in n years' time, we need to invest a certain sum *now* (year 0) at an interest rate of r% in order to obtain the required sum of money in the future.

For example, if we wish to have £14,641 in four years' time, how much money would we need to invest now at 10% interest per annum? This is the reverse of the situation described above.

Using our corresponding formula, S = X$(1 + r)^n$

where	X	=	the original sum invested
	r	=	10%
	n	=	4
	S	=	£14,641

£14,641	=	X$(1 + 0.1)^4$
£14,641	=	X $\times$ 1.4641

$$\therefore X = \frac{£14,641}{1.4641} = £10,000$$

£10,000 now, with the capacity to earn a return of 10% per annum, is the equivalent in value of £14,641 after four years. We can therefore say that **£10,000 is the present value of £14,641 at year 4, at an interest rate of 10%**.

10.2 Present value

The term **'present value'** simply means the amount of money which must be invested now for n years at an interest rate of r%, to earn a given future sum of money at the time it will be due.

10.3 The formula for discounting

Formula to learn

The discounting formula is

$$X = S \times \frac{1}{(1+r)^n}$$

where   S   is the sum to be received after n time periods
         X   is the present value (PV) of that sum
         r   is the rate of return, expressed as a proportion
         n   is the number of time periods (usually years).

The rate r is sometimes called a cost of capital.

Note that this equation is just a rearrangement of the compounding formula.

Example: discounting

(a)   Calculate the present value of £60,000 at year 6, if a return of 15% per annum is obtainable.
(b)   Calculate the present value of £100,000 at year 5, if a return of 6% per annum is obtainable.
(c)   How much would a person need to invest now at 12% to earn £4,000 at year 2 and £4,000 at year 3?

Solution

The discounting formula, $X = S \times \dfrac{1}{(1+r)^n}$ is required.

(a)   S   =   £60,000
       n   =   6
       r   =   0.15

BPP
PROFESSIONAL EDUCATION

$$PV = 60,000 \times \frac{1}{1.15^6}$$

$$= 60,000 \times 0.432$$
$$= £25,920$$

(b) $S = £100,000$
$n = 5$
$r = 0.06$

$$PV = 100,000 \times \frac{1}{1.06^5}$$

$$= 100,000 \times 0.747$$
$$= £74,700$$

(c) $S = £4,000$
$n = 2 \text{ or } 3$
$r = 0.12$

$$PV = (4,000 \times \frac{1}{1.12^2}) + (4,000 \times \frac{1}{1.12^3})$$

$$= 4,000 \times (0.797 + 0.712)$$
$$= £6,036$$

This calculation can be checked as follows.

	£
Year 0	6,036.00
Interest for the first year (12%)	724.32
	6,760.32
Interest for the second year (12%)	811.24
	7,571.56
Less withdrawal	(4,000.00)
	3,571.56
Interest for the third year (12%)	428.59
	4,000.15
Less withdrawal	(4,000.00)
Rounding error	0.15

Activity 4.10

The present value at 7% interest of £16,000 at year 12 is £ [   ]

BPP)))
PROFESSIONAL EDUCATION

chapter 5

Computer spreadsheets

Contents

1 Introduction

Much of the information used by management is analysed or presented using spreadsheets. This chapter is an introduction to the use of spreadsheets, including how to set up and use formulae to carry out calculations.

2 Spreadsheets

The vast majority of people who work in an accounting environment are required to use spreadsheets to perform their duties. They need to be able to produce clear, well-presented spreadsheets that utilise basic spreadsheet functions such as simple formulae.

2.1 What is a spreadsheet?

A spreadsheet is essentially an **electronic piece of paper** divided into **rows** (horizontal) and **columns** (vertical). The rows are numbered 1, 2, 3 . . . etc and the columns lettered A, B C . . . etc. Each individual area representing the intersection of a row and a column is called a 'cell'. A cell address consists of its row and column reference. For example, in the spreadsheet below the word Jan is in cell B2. The cell that the cursor is currently in or over is known as the 'active cell'.

The main examples of spreadsheet packages are Lotus 1 2 3 and Microsoft Excel. We will be referring to Microsoft Excel, as this is the most widely-used spreadsheet. A simple Microsoft Excel spreadsheet, containing budgeted sales figures for three geographical areas for the first quarter of the year, is shown below.

	A	B	C	D	E	F
1	BUDGETED SALES FIGURES					
2		Jan	Feb	Mar	Total	
3		£'000	£'000	£'000	£'000	
4	North	2,431	3,001	2,189	7,621	
5	South	6,532	5,826	6,124	18,482	
6	West	895	432	596	1,923	
7	Total	9,858	9,259	8,909	28,026	
8						

2.2 Why use spreadsheets?

Spreadsheets provide a tool for calculating, analysing and manipulating numerical data. Spreadsheets make the calculation and manipulation of data easier and quicker. For example, the spreadsheet above has been set up to calculate the totals in column E and row 7 **automatically.** If you changed your estimate of sales in February for the North region to £3,296, when you input this figure in cell C4 the totals (in E4, C7 and E7) would change accordingly.

2.3 Cell contents

The contents of any cell can be one of the following.

(a) **Text**. A text cell usually contains **words**. Numbers that do not represent numeric values for calculation purposes (eg a Part Number) may be entered in a way that tells Excel to treat the cell contents as text. To do this, enter an apostrophe before the number eg '451.

(b)   **Values**. A value is a **number** that can be used in a calculation.

(c)   **Formulae**. A formula **refers to other cells** in the spreadsheet, and performs some sort of computation with them. For example, if cell C1 contains the formula =A1-B1, cell C1 will display the result of the calculation subtracting the contents of cell B1 from the contents of cell A1. In Excel, a formula always begins with an equals sign: = . There are a wide range of formulae and functions available.

3 Spreadsheet formulae

3.1 Formula bar

The following illustration shows the formula bar.

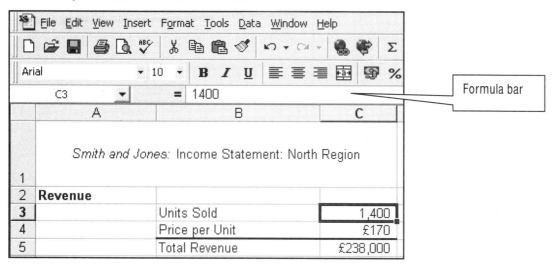

The formula bar allows you to see and edit the contents of the active cell. The bar also shows the cell address of the active cell (C3 in the example above).

3.2 Examples of spreadsheet formulae

Formulae in Microsoft Excel follow a specific syntax that includes an equal sign (=) followed by the elements to be calculated (the operands) and the calculation operators. Each operand can be a value that does not change (a constant value), a cell or range reference, a label, a name, or a worksheet function.

Formulae can be used to perform a variety of calculations. Here are some examples.

(a)   =C4*5. This formula **multiplies** the value in C4 by 5. The result will appear in the cell holding the formula.

(b)   =C4*B10. This **multiplies** the value in C4 by the value in B10.

(c)   =C4/E5. This **divides** the value in C4 by the value in E5. (* means multiply and / means divide by.)

(d)   =C4*B10-D1. This **multiplies** the value in C4 by that in B10 and then subtracts the value in D1 from the result. Note that generally Excel will perform multiplication and division before addition or subtraction. If in any doubt, use brackets: = (C4*B10)-D1.

(e)   =C4*117.5%. This **adds** 17.5% to the value in C4. It could be used to calculate a price including 17.5% VAT.

(f)   =(C4+C5+C6)/3. Note that the **brackets** mean Excel would perform the addition first. Without the brackets, Excel would first divide the value in C6 by 3 and then add the result to the total of the values in C4 and C5.

(g)   = 2^2 gives you 2 **to the power** of 2, in other words 2^2 . Likewise = 2^3 gives you 2 cubed and so on.

(h)   = 4^ (1/2) gives you the **square root** of 4. Likewise 27^(1/3) gives you the cube root of 27 and so on.

Excel calculates a formula from left to right, starting with the equals. You can control how calculation is performed by changing the syntax of the formula. For example, the formula =5+2*3 gives a result of 11 because Excel calculates multiplication before addition. Excel would multiply 2 by 3 (resulting in 6) and would then add 5.

You may use brackets to change the order of operations. For example =(5+2)*3 would result in Excel firstly adding the 5 and 2 together, then multiplying that result by 3 to give 21. In other words, Excel flows the normal mathematical order.

Activity 5.1

	A	B	C	D	E	F
1	BUDGETED SALES FIGURES					
2		Jan	Feb	Mar	Total	
3		£'000	£'000	£'000	£'000	
4	North	2,431	3,001	2,189	7,621	
5	South	6,532	5,826	6,124	18,482	
6	West	895	432	596	1,923	
7	Total	9,858	9,259	8,909	28,026	
8						

(a)   In the spreadsheet shown above, which of the cells have had a number typed in, and which cells display the result of calculations (ie which cells contain a formula)?

(b)   What formula would you put in each of the following cells?

(i)   Cell B7
(ii)   Cell E6
(iii)   Cell E7

(c)   If the February sales figure for the South changed from £5,826 to £5,731, what other figures would change as a result? Give cell references.

3.3 Relative and Absolute Cell references

We will explain this concept by using an example. Formulae in 'standard' form, for example the formula =SUM(B7:B9) located in cell B10, are said to be relative. This formula does not really mean 'add up the numbers in cells B7 to B9'; it actually means 'add up the numbers in the three cells above this one'. So, if this **relative** formula was copied to cell C15 it would become =SUM(C12:C14). Sometimes this automatic amendment to copied formulae may not be required. In this situation you should use **absolute** referencing.

If we insert a dollar sign $ before the column letter, this makes the column reference absolute. So, copying =(SUM$B7:$B9) from B10 to C15 would give =SUM($B12:$B14).

A dollar sign before the row number makes the row number absolute. So, copying =(SUMB$7:B$9) from B10 to C15 would give =SUM(C$7:C$9).

A dollar sign before the column letter and row number makes the complete cell reference absolute. So, copying =(SUM$B$7:$B9) from B10 to C15 would give =(SUM$B$7:$B$9).

You do not need to type the dollar signs, you can highlight the cell references you wish to make absolute and then press F4. This adds dollar signs to cell references in the formula, for example C31 would become $C$31. If you pressed F4 again, the reference becomes C$31. Press it again: the reference becomes $C31. Press it once more, and the simple relative reference is restored: C31.

4 Basic spreadsheet skills

In this section we explain some **basic spreadsheeting skills**. We give instructions for Microsoft Excel, the most widely used package. Our examples should be valid with all versions of Excel released since 1997. You should read this section while sitting at a computer and trying out the skills we describe, **'hands-on'**. Come back to this section later if you cannot do this right now.

4.1 Examples of useful spreadsheet skills

Start Microsoft Excel by double-clicking on the Excel **icon** or button (it will look like an X), or by choosing Excel from the **Start** menu (maybe from within the **Microsoft Office** option).

4.1.1 Moving about

The F5 key is useful for moving about large spreadsheets. If you press the function key **F5,** a **Go To** dialogue box will allow you to specify the cell address you would like to move to. Try this out.

Also experiment by holding down Ctrl and pressing each of the direction arrow keys in turn to see where you end up. Try using the **Page Up** and **Page Down** keys and also try **Home** and **End** and Ctrl + these keys. Try **Tab** and **Shift + Tab**, too. These are all useful shortcuts for moving quickly from one place to another in a large spreadsheet.

4.1.2 Editing cell contents

Suppose cell A2 currently contains the value 456. If you wish to **change the entry** in cell A2 from 456 to 123456 there are four options – as shown below.

(a)   Activate cell A2, **type** 123456 and press **Enter**. (To undo this and try the next option press **Ctrl + Z**: this will always undo what you have just done.)

(b)   **Double-click** in cell A2. The cell will keep its thick outline but you will now be able to see a vertical line flashing in the cell. You can move this line by using the direction arrow keys or the Home and the End keys. Move it to before the 4 and type 123. Then press Enter.

After you have tried this, press Ctrl + Z to undo it.

(c) **Click once** on the number 456 in the line that shows the active cell reference and cell contents at the top of the screen. Again you will get the vertical line and you can type in 123 before the 4. Then press Enter, then Ctrl + Z.

(d) Press the **function key F2**. The vertical line cursor will be flashing in cell A2 at the *end* of the figures entered there (after the 6). Press Home to get to a position before the 4 and then type in 123 and press Enter, as before.

4.1.3 Deleting cell contents

You may delete the contents of a cell simply by making the cell the active cell and then pressing **Delete**. The contents of the cell will disappear. You may also highlight a range of cells to delete and then delete the contents of all cells within the range.

For example, enter any value in cell A1 and any value in cell A2. Move the cursor to cell A2. Now hold down the **Shift** key (the one above the Ctrl key) and keeping it held down press the ↑ arrow. Cell A2 will stay white but cell A1 will go black. What you have done here is **selected** the range A1 and A2. Now press Delete. The contents of cells A1 and A2 will disappear.

4.1.4 Filling a range of cells

Start with a blank spreadsheet. Type the number 1 in cell A1 and the number 2 in cell A2. Now *select* cells A1: A2, this time by positioning the mouse pointer over cell A1, holding down the left mouse button and moving the pointer down to cell A2. When cell A2 goes black you can release the mouse button.

Now position the mouse pointer at the **bottom right hand corner** of cell A2. (You should be able to see a little black lump in this corner: this is called the **'fill handle'**.) When you have the mouse pointer in the right place it will turn into a black cross.

Hold down the left mouse button again and move the pointer down to cell A10. You will see an outline surrounding the cells you are trying to 'fill'.

Release the mouse button when you have the pointer over cell A10. You will find that the software **automatically** fills in the numbers 3 to 10 below 1 and 2.

Try the following variations of this technique.

(a) Delete what you have just done and type in **Jan** in cell A1. See what happens if you select cell A1 and fill down to cell A12: you get the months **Feb, Mar, Apr** and so on.

(b) Type the number 2 in cell A1. Select A1 and fill down to cell A10. What happens? The cells should fill up with 2's.

(c) Type the number 2 in cell A1 and 4 in cell A2. Then select A1: A2 and fill down to cell A10. What happens? You should get 2, 4, 6, 8, and so on.

(d) Try **filling across** as well as down. In Excel you can fill in any direction.

(e) What happens if you click on the bottom right hand corner using the **right mouse button**, drag down to another cell and then release the button? You should get a menu giving you a variety of different options for how you want the cells to be filled in.

4.1.5 The Sum button Σ

Start with a blank spreadsheet, and then enter the following figures in cells A1:B5.

	A	B
1	400	582
2	250	478
3	359	264
4	476	16
5	97	125

Make cell B6 the active cell and click *once* on the sum button (the button with a Σ symbol on the toolbar - the Σ symbol is the mathematical sign for 'the sum of'). A formula will appear in the cell saying =SUM(B1:B5). Above cell B6 you will see a flashing dotted line encircling cells B1:B5. Accept the suggested formula by hitting the Enter key. The formula =SUM(B1:B5) will be entered, and the number 1465 will be appear in cell B6.

Next, make cell A6 the active cell and **double-click** on the sum button. The number 1582 should show in cell A6.

4.1.6 Multiplication

Continuing on with our example, next select cell C1. Type in an = sign then click on cell A1. Now type in an **asterisk *** (which serves as a **multiplication sign**) and click on cell B1. Watch how the formula in cell C1 changes as you do this. (Alternatively you can enter the cell references by moving the direction arrow keys.) Finally press Enter. Cell C1 will show the result (232,800) of multiplying the figure in Cell A1 by the one in cell B1.

Your next task is to select cell C1 and **fill in** cells C2 to C5 automatically using the filling technique described earlier. If you then click on each cell in column C and look above at the line showing what the cell contains you will find that the software has automatically filled in the correct cell references for you: A2*B2 in cell C2, A3*B3 in cell C3 and so on.

(**Note**: The forward slash / is used to represent division in spreadsheet formulae).

4.1.7 Inserting columns and rows

Suppose we also want to add each row, for example cells A1 and B1. The logical place to do this would be cell C1, but column C already contains data. We have three options that would enable us to place this total in column C.

(a)   Highlight cells C1 to C5 and position the mouse pointer on one of the **edges**. (It will change to an arrow shape.) Hold down the **left** mouse button and drag cells C1 to C5 into column D. There is now space in column C for our next set of sums. Any **formulae** that need to be changed as a result of moving cells using this method should be changed **automatically** – but always check them.

(b)   The second option is to highlight cells C1 to C5 as before, position the mouse pointer anywhere **within** column C and click on the **right** mouse button. A menu will appear offering you an option **Insert...** . If you click on this you will be asked where you want to shift the cells that are being moved. In this case you want to move them to the *right* so choose this option and click on OK.

(c)   The third option is to **insert a whole new column**. You do this by clicking on the letter at the top of the column (here C) to highlight the whole of it then proceeding as in (b). The new column will be inserted to the left of the one you highlight.

You can now display the sum of each of the rows in column C.

You can also insert a **new row** in a similar way (or stretch rows).

(a)   To insert **one** row – for headings say – click on the row number to highlight it, click with the right mouse button and choose insert. One row will be inserted **above** the one you highlighted. Try putting some headings above the figures in columns A to C.

(b)   To insert **several** rows click on the row number **immediately below** the point where you want the new rows to appear and, holding down the left mouse button select the number of extra rows you want – rows 1, 2 and 3, say, to insert three rows above the current row 1. Click on the highlighted area with the right mouse button and choose insert.

4.1.8 Changing column width

You may occasionally find that a cell is not wide enough to display its contents. When this occurs, the cell displays a series of hashes ######. There are two options available to solve this problem.

(a)   One is to **decide for yourself** how wide you want the columns to be. Position the mouse pointer at the head of column A directly over the little line dividing the letter A from the letter B. The mouse **pointer** will change to a sort of **cross**. Hold down the left mouse button and, by moving your mouse, stretch Column A to the right, to about the middle of column D, until the words you typed fit. You can do the same for column B. Then make your columns too narrow again so you can try option (b).

(b)   Often it is easier to **let the software decide for you**. Position the mouse pointer over the little dividing line as before and get the cross symbol. Then double-click with the left mouse button. The column automatically adjusts to an appropriate width to fit the widest cell in that column.

You can either adjust the width of each column individually or you can do them all in one go. To do the latter click on the button in the top left hand corner to **select the whole sheet** and then **double-click** on just one of the dividing lines: all the columns will adjust to the **'best fit'** width.

4.1.9 Keyboard shortcuts and toolbar buttons

Finally a few tips to improve the **appearance** of your spreadsheets and speed up your work. To do any of the following to a cell or range of cells, first **select** the cell or cells and then:

(a)   Press Ctrl + B to make the cell contents **bold.**

(b)   Press Ctrl + I to make the cell contents *italic.*

(c)   Press **Ctrl + C** to **copy** the contents of the cells.

(d)   Move the cursor and press **Ctrl + V** to **paste** the cell you just copied into the new active cell or cells.

There are also **buttons** in the Excel toolbar (shown below) that may be used to carry out these and other functions. The best way to learn about these features is to use them - enter some numbers and text into a spreadsheet and experiment with keyboard shortcuts and toolbar buttons.

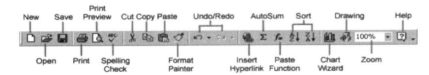

5 Spreadsheet format and appearance

It is important that the information provided in a spreadsheet is easy to understand. Good presentation can help people understand the contents of a spreadsheet.

5.1 Titles and labels

A spreadsheet should be headed up with a title which **clearly defines its purpose**. Examples of titles are follows.

  (a)   Trading, profit and loss account for the year ended 30 June 200X

  (b)   (i)   Area A: Sales forecast for the three months to 31 March 200X
        (ii)   Area B: Sales forecast for the three months to 31 March 200X
        (iii) Combined sales forecast for the three months to 31 March 200X

  (c)   Salesmen: Analysis of earnings and commission for the six months ended 30 June 200X

Row and **column** headings (or labels) should clearly identify the contents of the row/column. Any assumptions made that have influenced the spreadsheet contents should be clearly stated.

5.2 Formatting

There are a wide range of options available under the **Format** menu. Some of these functions may also be accessed through toolbar **buttons**. Formatting options include the ability to:

  (a)   Add **shading** or **borders** to cells.

  (b)   Use **different sizes of text** and different **fonts**.

  (c)   Choose from a range of options for presenting values, for example to present a number as a **percentage** (eg 0.05 as 5%), or with commas every third digit, or to a specified number of **decimal places** etc.

Experiment with the various formatting options yourself.

5.2.1 Formatting numbers

Most spreadsheet programs contain facilities for presenting numbers in a particular way. In Excel you simply select **Format** and then **Cells ...**to reach these options.

  (a)   **Fixed format** displays the number in the cell rounded off to the number of decimal places you select.

  (b)   **Currency format** displays the number with a '£' in front, with commas and not more than two decimal places, eg £10,540.23.

  (c)   **Comma format** is the same as currency format except that the numbers are displayed without the '£'.

  (d)   **General format** is the format assumed unless another format is specified. In general format the number is displayed with no commas and with as many decimal places as entered or calculated that fit in the cell.

  (e)   **Percent format** multiplies the number in the display by 100 and follows it with a percentage sign. For example the number 0.548 in a cell would be displayed as 54.8%.

  (f)   **Hidden format** is a facility by which values can be entered into cells and used in calculations but are not actually displayed on the spreadsheet. The format is useful for hiding sensitive information.

5.3 Gridlines

One of the options available under the **Tools**, **Options** menu, on the **View** tab, is an option to remove the gridlines from your spreadsheet.

Compare the following two versions of the same spreadsheet. Note how the formatting applied to the second version has improved the spreadsheet presentation.

	A	B	C	D	E	F
1	Sales team salaries and commissions - *200X*					
2	Name	Sales	Salary	Commi:	Total earnings	
3		£	£	£	£	
4	Northingto	284000	14000	5680	19680	
5	Souther	193000	14000	3860	17860	
6	Weston	12000	14000	240	14240	
7	Eastermar	152000	14000	3040	17040	
8						
9	Total	641000	56000	12820	68820	
10						

	A	B	C	D	E
1		*Sales team salaries and commissions - 200X*			
2	*Name*	*Sales*	*Salary*	*Commission*	*Total earnings*
3		£	£	£	£
4	Northington	284,000	14,000	5,680	19,680
5	Souther	193,000	14,000	3,860	17,860
6	Weston	12,000	14,000	240	14,240
7	Easterman	152,000	14,000	3,040	17,040
8					
9	Total	641,000	56,000	12,820	68,820
10					

PROFESSIONAL EDUCATION

Part B: Business English

BPP
PROFESSIONAL EDUCATION

chapter 6

Writing business English

Contents

1 Introduction

In business, you will need to be able to write reports, memos and business letters.

It is essential that you use 'professional business English' and avoid e-mail shorthand or texting language.

2 Writing business English

One of the commonest failings of students at any stage is poor English, so if you are a bit uncertain of your skills in this area you are probably in the majority.

To be brutally frank, people judge by appearances. If your written English is poor, people will think you are unintelligent. Rightly or wrongly this is a fact of life. If you do not try to do something about it, you will hinder your career progression.

If you think you need help in this area, read on. You will not be able to take in all the hints and rules that we give in one reading. You should keep these pages with you and use them as a source of reference.

2.1 Writing poor English

There are four common faults in writing a business letter or report.

(a) **Being too colloquial**, just writing down what you would **say** if you were speaking to the person you are writing to

(b) **Writing in note form**, leaving out words that you would not leave out in normal speech, let alone in formal writing

(c) **Bad spelling**

(d) **Bad punctuation**

In the remainder of this chapter we are going to go through some basic rules and some very common mistakes that people make. Some of this may take you back to primary school days, but we have tried to make the examples a little more relevant to your studies.

2.2 Sentences

Always write in full sentences. A sentence has the following characteristics.

(a) It starts with a capital letter and ends with a full stop.

(b) It must always have a minimum of one thing/person and one action (or one noun and one verb, to use the technical terms).

Clocks tick.

I am writing.

Most of the sentences you write will have an additional thing/person, with one of the things performing the action on the other one.

I am writing a book.

I am writing to you.

(c) Things or persons can be collections of words as well as single words. Though it might look more complicated the following sentence is in the standard form *person does thing.*

The senior manager of ABC Ltd has written a report on the future of the industry.

(d) There are two ways of looking at anything that happens.

    (i)   Things *perform* actions.
    (ii)   Actions *are performed by* things.

Method (i) is generally preferable in business writing.

(e) Sentences can, and usually will, be longer than the examples given so far. They can be joined up by words like *and* or *but* or *although,* or you can give extra information about something in the main part of your sentence using words like *who, which* or *that.*

As a general rule, in business communications, the simpler your sentences are the better. This means that you should keep them fairly short.

Try not to write sentences that are all the same length, however, because this is very monotonous to read.

2.3 Paragraphs

If you just write sentence after sentence with no breaks, your writing will be very tiring to read and difficult to follow. For this reason groups of sentences are split into paragraphs and there is a space between each paragraph.

A paragraph should have only one main idea. This may mean that it only has one sentence, or there may be additional sentences exploring the main idea, or leading up to the main idea. This paragraph that you are reading now has one main sentence (the first) and two additional sentences exploring the main idea.

In practice it is often difficult to decide where one main idea finishes and the next one starts. The rule again is to keep things short and simple but not to the extent that your writing gets monotonous.

In day to day business communications, which tend to be fairly short anyway, it will quite often be appropriate to have a new paragraph for each sentence. Most newspapers tend to be written in this style, too. In a 3,000 - 4,000 word report, however, this is liable to get very monotonous.

2.4 Brevity

Brevity is said to be the soul of wit. It is certainly essential in business writing. You must make your meaning clear, but you should use as few words as possible to do so. Superfluous words obscure the meaning and waste the reader's time.

Consider these sentences from a management text book and compare them with the edited versions.

Original sentences

- *A high staff turnover may be indicative of a wider problem such as poor morale.*

- *Identify the development areas that need to be addressed.*

- *Check to ensure that the activity has been carried out and successfully completed.*

- *The job description details the characteristics that a successful candidate would need to demonstrate.*

Edited sentences

- *A high staff turnover may indicate a wider problem such as poor morale.*

- *Identify the development areas to be addressed.*

- *Check that the activity has been carried out.*

- *The job description details the characteristics of a successful candidate.*

Overall, the word count has been reduced from 51 to 38: a 25% reduction.

It is actually quite difficult to write briefly and clearly. The secret is to **read what you have written** and ask yourself if it could be improved.

3 Common mistakes

3.1 A, an, the

These little words are the simplest in the language. They are so simple that you often leave them out in informal writing and in notes.

Do **not** leave them out in formal writing.

3.2 Etc, etc

Avoid *ie* (in other words) and *eg* (for example), and never use *etc* (and so on).

If you are tempted to use these abbreviations take note of the following points.

   (a)   To people who know better you will look very silly if you use *ie* when you mean *eg* or *eg* when you mean *ie*. This is a very common mistake.

       (i)   You use *ie* when you are *clarifying* what you have just said.

           ... any of the standard colours available, ie green, red or blue.

           This fell off the back of a lorry, ie it is stolen.

       (ii)   You use *eg* if you are only giving selected *examples* (or a single example) of what you have just said rather than a complete list.

           ... any colour you like, eg sea-green, pillar-box red, tartan, pink ... .

... retailers, eg Sainsbury's ...

To avoid mistakes do as we suggest initially: don't use these abbreviations at all!

(b) Either punctuate properly or don't punctuate at all. Do one or the other consistently.

i.e. e.g.   *etc.*   OR   *ie*   *eg*   *etc*

BUT NOT   *ie.*   *eg.*   *e.t.c.*

(c) When you write **etc** at the end of a list, you are saying that both you and the reader know perfectly well all the other items which are needed to make the list absolutely complete. The only occasion when this is likely to be true is if you have given the complete list earlier. If you are tempted to use *etc* ask yourself if you can think of any more items. If you can, write them down instead of *etc*. If you cannot, do not write *etc* hoping that readers will think you could if you wanted to. They will almost certainly assume the opposite.

(d) Do not forget that items in a simple list are separated by commas except for the last two which are joined by 'and'. If the items in a list consist of more than a couple of words, or if one of them includes the word 'and', use **semicolons** instead of commas. For example:

A competent payroll clerk should be able to deal with piecework pay; deduction of tax and national insurance; joiners and leavers; and preparation of P60s.

3.3 Get things right and do them properly

Often you will want to say something descriptive about the things or the actions in your sentences. You do this by using one or other of two types of *description word*, depending on whether you are describing a thing or an action. One of the most common mistakes that people make is to use the wrong sort of description word.

The basic rule is that if you are describing an *action* the word you use ends with *-ly*.

Example	Explanation
These figures are incorrect.	'incorrect' describes the figures
These figures have been added up incorrectly.	'incorrectly' describes the adding up
That is bad English.	'bad' describes the English
That is badly written.	'badly' describes the writing
Get things right	'right' describes the things
Do them properly	'properly' describes how they are done

Description words that describe *actions* usually say *how* the action is done or *where* it is done or *when* it is done.

3.4 Most common or commonest?

Do you say that something is *more common* than something else or do you say it is *commoner*? The basic rules for deciding whether to add *-er* and *-est* to a word or use *more* and *most* are as follows.

(a)   If the word has only one syllable add *-er* and *-est*: *harder, longer, biggest, highest* and so on.

(b)   If the word has two syllables and ends in *-y, -er, -le* or *-ow*, add *-er* and *-est*: *likeliest, happiest, lazier, idlest, cleverest, narrower* and so on. Also add *-er* and *-est* if using the *un-* form of these words: *unlikeliest, unhappier* and so on.

(c)   Otherwise use *more* and *most*: *more difficult, more probable, most intelligent, most infuriating* and so on.

With some words you can either add *-er* and *-est* or use *more* and *most* (*common* is such a word), but if you apply the rules above you should never make a mistake.

3.5 Who's who?

Sometimes you can find yourself using words like *he, she, it* and *them* (pronouns, if you want the technical term) so much in a passage of writing that it is not clear what they refer to.

For example, consider this:

Tom, Dick and Harry were talking about their work and Tom said to Dick that he thought he was great.

Does Tom think Dick is great? Or that he is great himself? Or is he saying that Dick thinks highly of himself or, perhaps, of Harry? Or is it that Tom thinks Harry appreciates Dick? There are even more possibilities than these.

You need to read your writing carefully to check whether it contains this sort of ambiguity. To get round the problem you usually have to identify one or more of the people or things involved, using a name or description instead of, or as well as, the word he, she or it.

Jo thought <u>his supervisor</u> was great. He also thought <u>he, Jo</u>, was great.

3.6 I and me

While we are on the subject of words like *he, she* and *it* we may as well remind you about *I* and *me*. Quite simply, use the form *me* if somebody else is doing the action to you.

The company gave Lucy and me a big pay rise.

The company is doing the giving.

If you are doing the action use the form *I*.

I got a big pay rise and so did Lucy.   OR   *Lucy and I got a big pay rise.*

Here it is you who is doing the getting. The question 'Who is doing the action?' is very often the key to a good sentence, as the next few paragraphs illustrate.

3.7 Who's doing what?

Which of the following sentences is correct?

1   *The best guide are accounting standards.*

2   *The problem here is the words are and is.*

_____

The words are and is are the problem. Do you make your action words (or verbs) singular or plural when the first thing is singular and the second thing is plural?

The answer is that it depends which comes first. Sentence 2 is the correct one. If you look carefully at sentence 2 and then go on to the sentence below it beginning 'The words ...' you will see that they say the same thing, except that the order of the words has been changed round. The use of the singular is or the plural are depends on whether what comes first is singular or plural.

If there are two things doing the action and one is singular and the other is plural what happens to the action word? For example is the following sentence correct?

References and an application form has been sent to Mr Slater.

If you think about it, Mr Slater will receive both the references and the form. In other words there are two things performing the action of being sent so the action word must be plural: in the sentence above has should say *have been sent*.

Be careful not to be distracted by words that just happen to come between the thing doing the action and the action word itself.

The source of the mistakes were not known.

It is tempting in a sentence like this to make the action word fit in with the word nearest to it (mistakes), but give it a moment's thought and you will realise that it is not the mistakes (plural) that are unknown but their source (singular): *were* should therefore be *was*.

If a word like *who* or *which* gets in the way be careful. Is this sentence correct?

An accountant is one of those professionals who helps to run businesses and gets well-paid for it.

In fact the words helps and gets are both wrong. It is professionals who help and professionals who get well-paid. The accountant is just one of these people.

3.8 Which hunting

Which is one of the most overused words in bad writing. Here is a simple explanation.

(a)   *The invoice <u>that</u> we sent you last week contained an error.*

   BUT

   I posted that transaction to the sales ledger, <u>which</u> was a mistake.

   Technically, *that* is used when it begins a series of words that *define* what has gone before. In the first example above the words beginning with *that* give information that distinguishes the invoice containing the error from any other invoice. In contrast *which* is used when the sentence changes direction slightly in order to complete the thought it expresses.

   This change is indicated by the comma that precedes *which*.

(b)   If it sounds better to join up the bits of your sentence with a simple *and* or *but* or to write two separate short sentences you should probably do so. Both of the following are correct but the second is better.

   You will be sent two invoices, <u>which</u> you may pay together if you wish.

You will be sent two invoices <u>but</u> you may pay both together if you wish.

Don't worry unduly about this: simply be aware that if which is badly used it can get you into all sorts of difficulties that could easily have been avoided.

3.9 Who and whom

Strictly, when *who* is the person having an action done to them the form to use is *whom.*

The customers to whom these invoices were sent have all complained.

If you are confident about using whom then do so by all means. In speech, though, you would probably have said The customers who these invoices were sent to have all complained. Likewise in modern business writing it is probably not worth worrying unduly about whom. So long as you are keeping things short and simple it will not offend many people if you break the rule.

A related problem is whether it is allowable to end a sentence with what is technically known as a *preposition*: a 'position' word like *to* or *with* or *from*. In general try to avoid doing so, but do not worry unduly about it. There is a famous example of how badly wrong you can go if you try too hard to avoid it.

That is something up with which I will not put.

This is taking the rules to extremes. It makes it harder, not easier, for people to follow your writing. In fact it is something that readers should not be expected to put up with!

3.10 Do you or are you doing?

What is the difference between *I write* and *I am writing*? This is a frequent problem for people who learned another language before they learned English, because other languages do not make a distinction.

Sometimes it doesn't matter which form you use, but sometimes it does. If you are not sure which is correct instinctively, follow these simple rules and you will never make a mistake.

(a) If you are actually doing the action at the time when you are saying that you are doing it, use the *I am doing...* form.

(b) If you do the thing as a normal ongoing part of your life but you are not actually doing it at the time when you are talking or writing use the *I do* form.

Here is an example.

We <u>are investigating</u> your complaint and will write to you again when we have completed our enquiries.

We <u>investigate</u> all complaints fully and offer compensation if we prove to be at fault.

Similar rules can be applied to *I was doing* and *I did* (the first takes you back to a time when the action was actually being done; the second makes you think that though someone did it in the past it is now finished) but in this case either form is usually acceptable.

3.11 To boldly go

One of the forms of an action word is the *to* form: *to do, to calculate, to be, to decide* and so on. The *to* should be regarded as something that cannot be separated from the main action word. You do not write *to quickly calculate*. The correct form is *to calculate quickly*. This rule is based on Latin grammar, so it is really quite obsolete and shouldn't be followed slavishly in English. Most people break this rule in everyday speech and many people break it in their writing. However many others – quite possibly including some of the people that you write to – get annoyed by it. The safest option, therefore, is not to break the rule.

It is sometimes better to avoid the problem by changing the *to* form to something else.

We used to regularly send out statements, but this tends to get neglected now.

You could correct this by changing it to: *We used to send out statements regularly ... .* This is fine, but another possibility, if you wanted to leave *regularly* where it is, would be the following.

At one time we regularly sent out statements ...

3.12 Going too boldly

Never write *to* when what you mean is *too*. If your work is typed up always check that the typist has not typed *to* when you want *too*. This point is made again in the section on spelling but it is such a common mistake that it is worth giving you advance warning.

3.13 Try to get it right

You might often say to someone *I'm going to try and do that.* This is wrong because *and* is a word used to join up two separate things, whereas the *trying* and the *doing* are not two separate things. What you mean is that you are going to *try to do* whatever it is.

RIGHT	*Go and see what the matter is*	Going *and* seeing are two different things
WRONG	*Try and improve your writing skills*	Trying *to* improve is all one action

3.14 Should have

It is very easy to write *I should of done that by half past three.* You write this because in terms of pronunciation it is very close to what you say. It is never, ever correct, though, whatever your ears tell you.

What you really mean is *I should have done that ... .* The same problem arises and the same mistake is often made with *could*.

WRONG   *I could of finished that if the phone had not rung.*
RIGHT   *I could have finished that if the phone had not rung.*

3.15 Off with of

Since we are on the subject of *of* it is worth saying that just because you go *down to* the shops or *out of* the country or *up to* someone in the street, you do not get *off of* a bus. The word *off* is always quite happy on its own: you *get off a bus*. It is never correct to write *off of*, so you do not *collect the papers off of Mr Jones*, you collect them *from* Mr Jones.

3.16 Should and would

Since we are also on the subject of *should* it is worth mentioning the conventional way to ask someone to do something in business writing.

I <u>should</u> be grateful if you <u>would</u> settle this account.

Note that should is used with I and would is used with you. This is because should has the sense of ought to and would has the sense of be willing: using should and would like this is just a way of being polite. However so many people write I would be grateful nowadays that this, too, has become perfectly acceptable.

3.17 Their, there and they're

A common mistake is to use *their* when you mean *there* or using *they're* when you mean *their* or any other permutation of this error. Always check your writing to make sure that you have got these words right. This is not just a spelling problem: the three words have completely different meanings.

For a start you can make life a little easier for yourself by not using the form *they're* (they are) in formal writing: then there is one fewer to get wrong.

You probably know which spelling is right in different contexts, but it is very easy to write the wrong one as a slip of the pen. Here are some checks you can carry out to avoid this.

Their   in front of word is a neater way of writing *belonging to them* after it. If your sentence becomes nonsense when you cross out the word *their* and put in the words *belonging to them* you have the wrong word.

     Which of the following sentences is wrong?

     Students should always check there writing for common mistakes.

     Their is a good reason for checking words like this.

     The first sentence could be reworded: 'Students should always check the writing **belonging to them** for common mistakes'. The word there should therefore be spelled their. In the second sentence you cannot fit in the words belonging to them at all: it doesn't make sense. The word their should therefore be spelled there. Both of the sentences are wrong.

There   is the word to use if the next word is *is* or *are*. *There* can often be thought of as a similar word to *here*: in fact of course, it is just *here* with a *t* in front, and it indicates that something exists.

     There are the papers you asked for.   *Here are the papers ...*

     There are six students who always get this wrong and *Six students exist who ...*
     they will have to pay me £5 every time they do it in
     future!

PROFESSIONAL EDUCATION

You probably think that we have made a bit of a meal of this simple point. If so, we challenge you never to make mistakes with these words again!

4 Punctuation

4.1 Capitals

Use a capital letter only in the following situations.

(a)   At the beginning of a sentence

(b)   For names of people and institutions: Peter, Jo, Nicole, Barclays Bank plc, Berisford Limited, the Foreign Office

(c)   For titles: Inspector Morse, Sir Humphrey Appleby, Mr Gomez

(d)   For places and nationalities: Manchester, Japan, Italian

(e)   Where convention demands it: I, God. (Not using capitals for *plc* is also a convention)

Do not use capital letters otherwise. For example the following (taken from a piece of writing produced by an AAT student) is wrong.

At the end of the day Invoices and Statements are run off on the Printer.

The only capital letter that is correct here is the one at the beginning of the sentence: invoices, statements and printer are general words, not names of things that are special to this particular accounting department. Capitals where they are not needed distract and irritate your readers.

4.2 Consistency

There are, however, some circumstances in which it is neither right nor wrong to use capital letters. For example you might be inclined to use capital letters for someone's job title (*Mr Akashi, the Sales Director*) or for the name of a department (*the Purchase Ledger Department*). Whatever decision you make about capitals in these cases you must be consistent within a single document: either *always* use capitals whenever you refer to them or *never* use capitals, but do not do one thing in one paragraph and another in the next.

4.3 Quotation marks

The main thing to remember about quotation marks is that you should hardly ever use them in business writing.

(a)   It is a very common and very irritating mistake to use them when you are not sure that you have chosen the right word, or when you think you are using a word in a colloquial way. It is also common, but wrong, to use them when you are referring to something that you think is unusual in context, or when you are trying to emphasise something. Avoid these errors in the following ways.

(i)   Choose another word that is more appropriate.

(ii)   Do not use highly colloquial expressions in formal written English. Ask yourself if you would use the expression if you were talking to a senior person in your organisation and wanted to make a good impression. (Would you say to your company's managing director 'Yo, MD! What's happening?' If not, do not use the expression.)

(iii)   If your reader will understand the word you are using, even though it seems a bit wacky, there is no need to use quotation marks. (Find the example in the preceding sentence.)

If you are unsure, just consider whether quotation marks will *help* your reader. Putting them round the word 'wacky' does not help anybody to understand what it means. Quotation marks do not turn informal words into formal words.

(iv)   Quotation marks are *never* used for emphasis. Use *italics* for emphasis if typing and <u>underline</u> the word if writing by hand.

(b)   The only circumstances in which quotation marks *must* be used are these.

(i)   Use them when you are quoting the words that someone actually said.

'I'm fed up with students who put quotation marks all over the place', said the tutor.

One commentator was bullish about the prospects for accounting technicians: 'This new emphasis on communication skills could mean that AAT members become one of the highest paid groups in society.'

It will be fairly rare for you to quote direct speech in business communications.

(ii)   Use them when you are discussing a word or phrase *as a word or phrase*, probably prior to explaining its meaning. Really this is just a variation on the use of quotation marks for quotations.

This technique is known as 'double entry', and it involves ...

The term 'double entry' means ...

(c)   In BPP books we always use single quotation marks unless there is another set within the first set. If this happens the second set are double quotation marks.

The lecturer said 'This technique is known as "double entry", and it involves ...'

In other books, and as a general rule in newspapers, you might see the opposite approach, with double being the more frequent. Either approach is acceptable as long as you consistently follow one or the other throughout a piece of writing.

4.4 Apostrophes

In modern English apostrophes are used for two different purposes.

(a)   To show that something belongs to somebody or something: *employees' pay records* (meaning the *pay records of employees*).

(b)   To show that a letter has been missed out in a word such as *haven't* (short for *have not*) or *they're* (short for *they are*).

4.4.1 's or s'

If the word is plural the apostrophe comes after the *s*. If the word is singular the apostrophe comes before the *s*. This is simple enough but people very often get it wrong. This is probably because they do not check. The rule, if you do not want people to think you are thick, is: *always check that your apostrophes are in the right place!*

4.4.2 Do'nt and Don't

It is best not to use forms like *don't* and *isn't* and *aren't* in formal writing. If you use them in informal communications, get the apostrophe in the right place. It goes in the place where the letter has been omitted. For example *don't* is short for *do not*: the apostrophe takes the place of the missing letter *o*.

4.4.3 Its and it's

These two words do not mean the same thing. You will always pick the right one, though if you simply remember that an apostrophe between two letters means that something has been left out between those two letters. Test by inserting the word *is* and seeing if your sentence still makes sense.

It's time you got to grips with double entry	MEANS	*It <u>is</u> time ...*
It's a sunny day today	MEANS	*It <u>is</u> a sunny day ..*
Tell me the account code and its balance	DOES NOT MEAN	*... and it <u>is</u> balance.*

As we have already said, an even easier way to get this right is to avoid using the form *it's* completely. Say *it is* instead.

4.4.4 Whose and who's

Apply the same rule as you apply for *its* and *it's*. If you can insert the word *is* and your sentence still makes sense the form to use is *who's*. Better, use *who is*.

4.4.5 Shop windows

People who write things in huge white letters on shop windows appear to have learned this skill at a special school that required them to make at least one mistake per window. How often have you seen something like this?

HUNDRED'S
OF
BARGAIN'S!!

Both of the apostrophes here are wrong. *Hundreds* and *bargains* are just the plural of *hundred* and *bargain*.

It is probably the word *of* that causes the confusion. If you are guilty of this error try to remember the following examples.

Dozens of students

Dozens of students' pay packets

Whenever *'s* or *s'* is used there *must* be something else in the sentence that belongs to the word with the apostrophe. In the first sentence the students are penniless so they have no apostrophe. In the second sentence the pay packets belong to them so they celebrate by adding an apostrophe.

4.5 Commas

Some people use commas to mark places in their sentences where they would pause for breath. This is totally wrong. The people who read your report will breathe as and when they need to: otherwise you would be able to suffocate people by writing extra long sentences.

(You may find that people in authority (your boss, your tutor) believe that punctuation marks are breathing marks, probably because that is what they were taught at school. Tell them to buy a little Penguin book by E V Carey called *Mind the Stop* if they do not believe BPP.)

Commas are used to make the logic of your sentence clearer. Since you will be writing relatively short simple sentences in all your business communications you should not need to use them very much at all.

Here are some simple rules for using commas. These cover the most common uses.

(a) Use commas in lists of items.

... red, white, blue and green.

... main ledger, sales ledger and purchase ledger.

The usual convention is not to put a comma before *and* and the last item, the argument being that the other commas are used in place of *and*. Sometimes this rule may need to be broken to make things clear, though:

... accounting firms such as Deloitte Touche, Baker Tilly, and Ernst and Young.

Without the comma a reader who is not familiar with these names might think that there was a firm called Baker Tilly and Ernst and Young.

(b) Use commas when there are bits of your sentence that could be missed out without making the sentence incomplete.

Debits, <u>which go on the left</u>, are assets of the business.

He said that debits go on the right, <u>which is incorrect</u>.

Mrs Chomsky, <u>one of our leading customers</u>, has cancelled her order.

Here you could miss out the words that are underlined and still have complete sentences.

There are sometimes odd individual words which you could leave out without damaging the sense of your sentence, but putting commas round them is overdoing it.

The payroll records, which were usually kept in the Personnel Department, had completely vanished.

Here you could miss out the words *usually* and *completely* but to put commas round them would distract your reader unnecessarily. The logic of the sentence is clear without them.

(c)   Use commas between bits of your sentence that could stand alone as independent sentences but which happen to be joined together with a connecting word. This is usually only necessary with fairly long sentences.

It was suggested that the discrepancy had occurred because entries in the accounting records for the second half of the year had been posted to the wrong accounts, but this proved not to be the source of the error once a more thorough investigation had been carried out.

The general rule, with the exceptions above, is to write simple sentences and use commas as little as possible.

4.6 Exclamation marks

Do not use exclamation marks in formal business writing. In informal writing there is no reason to use more than one.

4.7 Colons: introductions

The colon is two full stops, one on top of the other. You might want to use this occasionally to introduce things.

There are two types of accounting entry: debits and credits.

You may sometimes see a colon with a dash after it (:-). This is old-fashioned. You may find that older people use it. The dash is not necessary, so leave it out.

It is very easy to type a semi-colon (;) when you mean to type a colon (:) because the two are on the same key on a typewriter. Be aware of this and check carefully that writing that has been typed up has the punctuation mark you intended.

4.8 Separations and semi-colons

A semi-colon is a comma with a full stop on top of it. You might want to use these in lists where each item in the list is more than a few words, especially if there are also commas within items in the list.

Attending the meeting were: the managing director, who did not vote; Mr Smith, representing his wife; various small shareholders, most of whom wanted to raise specific issues; and a large man, who was sheltering from the rain.

It is unlikely that you would want to write like this in a business context. It is usually clearer and simpler to have separate lines for each thing in the list.

The meeting was attended by the following people.

- *The managing director, who did not vote*
- *Mr Smith, representing his wife*
- *Various small shareholders, most of whom wanted to raise specific issues*
- *A large man, who was sheltering from the rain*

4.9 Dashes

The dash is a multi-purpose punctuation mark and because of this it can make your writing sloppy – you can easily end up dashing about all over the place – not having a clear idea of where your sentence is going – not knowing quite where to finish – and leaving your reader in doubt as to what the point of your sentence was in the first place – if there was a point.

Dashes are fine if you know how to use them correctly. On the other hand anything you can do with a dash you can do equally well with other punctuation marks. It is probably best to avoid the problems and dangers by not using them at all.

4.10 Brackets

Brackets are used to include bits of extra information within the main sentence. The rules to remember are as follows.

(a)   Think of brackets as a form of double entry. For every opening bracket there must be an equal and opposite closing bracket. When you are checking your writing, the first thing you should do when you see an opening bracket is look for the closing one.

(b)   If there are too many brackets you will confuse your reader. Try to have no more than one set of brackets per sentence.

(c)   It should be possible to cross out the part of your sentence that is bracketed without upsetting the sense of the main part of the sentence.

Which of the following sentences is correctly punctuated?

This is the main (not the bracketed part) of the sentence.

This is the main (not the bracketed) part of the sentence.

If you cross out the bracketed part of the first sentence you are left with *This is the main of the sentence.* This does not make sense. The second version is the correct one. You should always check that you would be left with a full sentence if you cross out the part you have put in brackets.

4.11 Full stops, commas and brackets

The rules are simple.

(a)   If the bracketed part of a sentence is right at the end of the sentence the full stop comes *after* the closing bracket (like this). The full stop is normally part of the main sentence, not the bracketed part (see (d)).

(b)   Never put a comma, a colon or a semi-colon before an opening or closing bracket. Both of the commas in the following example are wrong and should be deleted.

... the sales ledger, (part of the accounting system,)

(c)   Commas can come after a closing bracket. As usual, try crossing out the bracketed part: if the comma that follows it would be necessary in the main sentence it is correct.

Dogs (which have four legs), ducks (which have two), and spiders (which have eight) were all on the menu that evening.

(d)   If you put brackets round an entire sentence the sentence should begin with a capital letter and end with a full stop, just like any other sentence.

(The whole of this sentence is in brackets.)

It is unusual to put brackets round a whole sentence.

5 Spelling problems

A lot of bad spellers could very easily be good spellers. These are people who know there are rules about, say, dropping the *e* at the end of a word when *-ing* is added to it (*care/caring*), or doubling the *l* when a word ending in *-ful* has *-ly* added to it (*careful/carefully*). Troubles start when people forget that there are exceptions to the rules, or they get confused about when to apply the rules, or they apply them too enthusiastically.

Unfortunately there is no easy way to improve your spelling. The most pleasurable way is to read a great deal: subconscious learning is probably the main way that you have learned to spell over the years. The problem is that this process works relatively slowly.

The most difficult way to improve your spelling is to learn what is called the **etymology** of English words: that is, how they are derived from old English, old Norse, French, Latin, German and so on. If you were to do this you would realise that there are good historical reasons for words having the spellings they have today, but again it would take you years to develop the expertise.

The compromise method is to learn and remember some basic rules and to learn any individual words that you have difficulty with off by heart. You might find it more acceptable to think of this as solving problems rather than learning rules.

On the following pages we set out some basic spelling rules.

Do not try to learn the table in one sitting.

Try to use it actively. Photocopy it and carry it around with you. Perhaps try to conquer one spelling problem a day and try to find examples of the rule or hint in anything you read that day. The next day, besides conquering a new problem, go over some of the other rules that you have already learned to fix them in your long-term memory. If you follow this timetable diligently you should find that your spelling improves dramatically and permanently.

5.1 Computer spell checking

Any decent word processing package includes a built-in dictionary. If you type something on a word processor you can then click on a button and the program will work through your document pausing at any word that does not appear in its dictionary and offering you the opportunity to correct your spelling or choose an alternative word.

If you have such a tool available you would be foolish not to use it. Make it your habit always to use the spell checking facility just before you close a document.

Remember, on the other hand, that there are certain mistakes that the spell check does not pick up. For example, if you type *form* but meant to type *from* the computer will not recognise your mistake. All it is doing is seeing if the words you have typed are spelled like that in the dictionary. Other examples are typing *i* when you mean *it* (the computer thinks you mean *I*) or typing *n* when you mean *in* or *on* (because individual letters of the alphabet are valid entries in the dictionary).

You cannot rely on the computer to do all your spelling for you or to correct badly written sentences. In other words, spell checking should not be regarded as a substitute for checking through a piece of word processing material on paper with the naked eye.

5.2 Basic good spelling

Problem	Rule or hint	Examples	Exceptions
Short words	Double the last letter when adding an ending. There are many exceptions, though: these just have to be learned.	bat/batted, drop/dropping, occur/occurring, omit/omitted	debit/debited, credit/credited bus/buses great/greater
-able	Try to pronounce words with this ending as they are spelled whenever you see them.		
-al	Words ending with single -l have ll when -ly is added.	real becomes really, national becomes nationally	
-ance, -ant	Try to pronounce words with these endings as they are spelled whenever you see them.		
-c	Add k if using -ing or -ed with a word that ends with c.	panic, panicking	
-cede	This is the normal spelling for words that end in this sound. There are only four exceptions: these are given opposite and you should learn them by heart.	concede, precede, recede	exceed proceed succeed supersede
-ch	Words ending in -ch have a plural ending in -es.	church, churches	
check	This word means to examine the accuracy of something.	Always check that you have not written cheque when you mean check!	
cheque	This word means a written order to the bank to pay a stated sum.	Always check that you have not written check when you mean cheque!	

Problem	Rule or hint	Examples	Exceptions
dis-	Just add dis and leave the rest of the word unchanged. Only use ss if the word itself begins with s.	disappear, displease, dissimilar	
-ei-	This is the correct spelling after a c (but see -ie-).	receipt	species
-ence, -ent	Try to pronounce words with these endings as they are spelled whenever you see them.		
fore-	This means 'before'. Do not confuse it with for- at the beginning of a word, which has other meanings.	forecast, forewarn forget, forbid forego means 'go before' forgo means 'go without'	
-fs	Words ending in -f or -fe generally have an -s added in the plural. Exceptions change the -f to -ves (they are spelled as they are pronounced).	beliefs, chiefs, proofs, safes	halves, knives, leaves, lives, loaves, selves, wives
-ful	Words ending with single -l have ll when -ly is added.	careful becomes carefully	
-ible	Try to pronounce words with this ending as they are spelled whenever you see them.		
-ie-	The most famous spelling rule is: I before E except after C. (C + EI is the same rule for accountants).	yuppies, receive, receipt, piece	foreign, either, counterfeit, forfeit, seize, weir, weird, neighbour, species
-ie	-ie changes to -y when -ing is added. It drops the e when -ed is added.	lie, lying, lied	
-ise or -ize	There is no rule. If in doubt use -ise.	advertise, advise	American spelling and some English writers use both. For example organize is common in UK newspapers.
-ll	Change a double -ll to single -l when the word forms part of a longer word. Contrast this with the rules for -al and -ful.	full, well, till become handful, welcome, until	illness, tallness, farewell

Problem	Rule or hint	Examples	Exceptions
mis-	Just add mis. Leave the rest of the word unchanged. Only use ss if the word itself begins with s.	misunderstand, mistake, misspell	
-ness	Use -nn- if the word to which -ness is added already ends in n.	keen, keenness, green, greenness	
-oe	Always keep the e unless the added ending begins with e.	hoe, hoes, hoeing, hoed	
-oes	Most words that end in -o becomes -oes in the plural. There are several common exceptions to learn, though.	echoes, vetoes, tomatoes, potatoes	zeros, provisos, photos, radios, pianos
-our	Drop the -u- when an ending is added.	humour, humorous, honour, honorary	honourable
-s, -sh	Words ending in -s or -sh have a plural ending in -es.	boss, bosses, dress, dresses. dish, dishes	
-ss	Keep ss if adding an ending.	assess, assessment, discuss, discussion	
too	This word means either 'also' or 'more than is desirable'. Check that you have not written to when you mean too.	This is too difficult. I want to win the lottery, too.	
-ves	See -fs.		
-x	Words ending in -x have a plural ending in -es.	box, boxes	
-y	Change -y to -i if the next letter is not a vowel (a,e,i,o,u).	beauty, beautiful, easy, easily	
-y	Words ending in -y change to -ies in the plural.	company, companies, diary, diaries, party, parties	Words ending in -ay, -ey, -oy, -uy: days, keys, toys, buys
–z	Words ending in –z have a plural ending in –es	fizz, fizzes	

PROFESSIONAL EDUCATION

Examples of business communications

Contents

1 Introduction

During the course of your exams, you will be asked to produce memos, reports and business letters. Do you understand the differences?

2 Memos

Memos are short, informal replies and are usually made to colleagues or management within the business. A memo usually has the following format.

MEMORANDUM

To:
From:
Date:
Subject

Example of a memo

The Chairman of Fellows plc needs to tell the payroll department that a director has been given an increase in salary.

FELLOWS PLC

MEMORANDUM

To: Payroll
From: Chairman
Date: 30.04.X4
Subject   Increase in director's salary

Peter Piper's salary is to increase from £25,000 pa to £29,000 pa with effect from 1st May 20X4

Chairman

You should note the following points.

(a)   The memo should show to whom it is addressed (Payroll).

(b)   The memo should show who sent it (Chairman).

(c)   The memo should be dated.

(d)   The subject should be shown clearly.

(e)   The memo is short and to the point. In this case, it is one sentence. However memos can be longer and can run to two or three paragraphs.

(f)   Memos are usually signed by the sender.

Unlike letters, there is no need to start with 'Dear' or to end with 'yours sincerely' or something similar. A memo is completely informal but do not fall into the trap of using text language or abbreviations. A memo must be written in business English.

Activity 7.1

The chairman of Fellows plc is Ashram Kahn. You are the payroll clerk, Chan Yuan. You have received the chairman's memo of 30 April 20X4. However Peter Piper's salary is already £30,000 pa, not £25,000. Complete the following memo informing Ashram Kahn of this fact and asking him for revised instructions. Today's date is 1st May 20X4.

FELLOWS PLC

MEMORANDUM

To:
From:
Date:
Subject

3 Reports

Reports are usually longer than memos. They may contain an analysis of a situation and recommended courses of action. They are more formal than memos.

In exams, you are quite often given a set of accounts and asked to prepare a report to the directors or bank. The report starts with similar information to a memo ie who it is addressed to; who it is from; date and subject matter.

The report should start with an introduction summarising what you have been asked to do. The body of the report should be divided into subject section and there should be a conclusion. If there are calculations to backup the report, these should be shown in an appendix at the end.

Example of a report

REPORT

To: Finance Director
From: Management accountant
Subject: *Performance of Laurie plc 20X0 to 20X2*

I have been asked to analyse the performance of Laurie plc over the past 3 years and to highlight areas requiring further investigation.

An appendix is attached to this report which shows the ratios calculated as part of the performance review.

Performance review

Profitability

The gross profit margin has remained relatively static over the three year period, although it has risen by approximately 1% in 20X2. ROCE, while improving very slightly in 20X1 to 21.5% has dropped dramatically in 20X2 to 17.8%. The net profit margin has also fallen in 20X2, in spite of the improvement in the gross profit margin. This marks a rise in expenses which suggests that they are not being well controlled. The utilisation of assets compared to the turnover generated has also declined reflecting the drop in trading activity between 20X1 and 20X2.

Trading levels

It is apparent that there was a dramatic increase in trading activity between 20X0 and 20X1, but then a significant fall in 20X2. Turnover rose by 17% in 20X1 but fell by 7% in 20X2. The reasons for this fluctuation are unclear. It may be the effect of some kind of one-off event, or it may be the effect of a change in product mix. Whatever the reason, it appears that improved credit terms granted to customers (debtors payment period up from 46 to 64 days) has not stopped the drop in sales.

Working capital

Both the current ratio and quick ratio demonstrate an adequate working capital situation, although the quick ratio has shown a slight decline. There has been an increased investment over the period in stocks and debtors which has been only partly financed by longer payment periods to trade creditors and a rise in other creditors (mainly between 20X0 and 20X1).

Capital structure

The level of gearing of the company increased when a further £64m was raised in long term loans in 20X1 to add to the £74m already in the balance sheet. Although this does not seem to be a particularly high level of gearing, the debt/equity ratio did rise from 18.5% to 32.0% in 20X1. The interest charge has risen to £19m from £6m in 20X0. The 20X1 charge was £15m, suggesting that either the interest rate on the loan is flexible, or that the full interest charge was not incurred in 20X1. The new long-term loan appears to have funded the expansion in both fixed and current assets in 20X1.

Conclusion

Areas for further investigation include the following.

(i) *Long-term loan*

There is no indication as to why this loan was raised and how it was used to finance the business. Further details are needed of interest rate(s), security given and repayment dates.

(ii)   *Trading activity*

The level of sales has fluctuated in quite a strange way and this requires further investigation and explanation. Factors to consider would include pricing policies, product mix, market share and any unique occurrence which would affect sales.

(iii)   *Further breakdown*

It would be useful to break down some of the information in the financial statements, perhaps into a management accounting format. Examples would be:

(1)   sales by segment, market or geographical area;
(2)   cost of sales split, into raw materials, labour and overheads;
(3)   stocks broken down into raw materials, work in progress and finished goods;
(4)   expenses analysed between administrative expenses, sales and distribution costs.

(iv)   *Accounting policies*

Accounting policies may have a significant effect on certain items. In particular, it would be useful to know what the accounting policies are in relation to intangible assets (and what these assets consist of), and whether there has been any change in accounting policies.

(v)   *Dividend policy*

The company has maintained the level of dividend paid to shareholders (although it has not been raised during the three year period). Presumably the company would have been able to reduce the amount of long-term debt taken on if it had retained part or all of the dividend during this period. It would be interesting to examine the share price movement during the period and calculate the dividend cover.

APPENDIX

Ratio	Working	20X0	20X1	20X2
Gross profit margin	(1)	34.0%	34.3%	35.4%
ROCE	(2)	21.1%	21.5%	17.8%
Profit margin	(3)	11.9%	12.4%	11.4%
Assets turnover	(4)	1.78	1.73	1.56
Gearing ratio	(5)	15.6%	24.3%	23.6%
Debt/equity ratio	(6)	18.5%	32.0%	30.9%
Interest cover	(7)	16.7	8.1	5.5
Current ratio	(8)	3.0	2.8	2.7
Quick ratio	(9)	1.2	1.1	1.1
Debtor's payment period (days)	(10)	46	52	64
Stock turnover period (days)	(11)	156	171	182
Creditor's turnover period	(12)	35	42	46

Workings (all in £m)

		20X0	20X1	20X2
1	Gross profit margin	$\dfrac{286}{840}$	$\dfrac{336}{981}$	$\dfrac{323}{913}$
2	ROCE *	$\dfrac{100}{473}$	$\dfrac{122}{568}$	$\dfrac{104}{584}$
3	Profit margin	$\dfrac{100}{840}$	$\dfrac{122}{981}$	$\dfrac{104}{913}$
4	Assets turnover	$\dfrac{840}{473}$	$\dfrac{981}{568}$	$\dfrac{913}{584}$
5	Gearing ratio	$\dfrac{74}{74 + 399}$	$\dfrac{138}{138 + 430}$	$\dfrac{138}{138 + 446}$
6	Debt/equity ratio	$\dfrac{74}{399}$	$\dfrac{138}{430}$	$\dfrac{138}{446}$
7	Interest cover	$\dfrac{100}{6}$	$\dfrac{122}{15}$	$\dfrac{104}{19}$
8	Current ratio	$\dfrac{394}{133}$	$\dfrac{502}{180}$	$\dfrac{506}{186}$
9	Quick ratio	$\dfrac{157}{133}$	$\dfrac{199}{180}$	$\dfrac{212}{186}$
10	Debtors' payment period	$\dfrac{105}{840} \times 365$	$\dfrac{141}{981} \times 365$	$\dfrac{160}{913} \times 365$
11	Stock turnover period	$\dfrac{237}{554} \times 365$	$\dfrac{303}{645} \times 365$	$\dfrac{294}{590} \times 365$
12	Creditors' payment period	$\dfrac{53}{554} \times 365$	$\dfrac{75}{645} \times 365$	$\dfrac{75}{590} \times 365$

* ROCE has been calculated here as:

$$\frac{\text{Profit on ordinary activities before interest and taxation (PBIT)}}{\text{Capital employed}}$$

where capital employed = shareholders' funds plus creditors falling due after one year and any long-term provision for liabilities and charges. It is possible to calculate ROCE using net profit after taxation and interest, but this admits variations and distortions into the ratio which are not affected by *trading* activity.

Note. You may not understand the comments at this stage of your studies, but the important thing is to note the structure of the report.

3.1 Planning an exam answer

If you are asked to produce a report, prepare an answer plan as follows.

(a)   Read the question requirements.

(b)   Skim through the question to obtain an overview.

(c)   Read through the question carefully, underlining any key words.

(d)   Set out the headings for the main part of your answer, leaving plenty of space to insert points within the headings.

(e)   Jot down points to make within these headings and underline those points you wish to expand upon.

(f)   Write your full answer and include all numerical calculations in an Appendix.

4 Business letters

A business letter is ore formal than a memo and usually much shorter than a report. Ideally it will cover just one topic.

Example: Business letter

An example of a business letter involving a debtor is set out below. Britton Trading Co plc has received a complaint from one of the firm's regular customers, UK Freight plc. UK Freight have received a statement indicating that payment of their account is overdue and that settlement must be made immediately. The amount stated to be outstanding is £2,340.20. UK Freight plc says that a cheque for this amount was paid on 23 August 20X3 but no acknowledgement of receipt was received.

Investigations have revealed that an incorrect ledger entry was made on 26 August 20X3. Payment of £2,340.20 was actually credited to the account of UK Carriage plc. August was a month in which there were staff changes in the office.

BRITTON TRADING CO PLC
WOLVERHAMPTON
WEST MIDLANDS

UK Freight plc
Tingeley Street
MANCHESTER
M12 4RS

22 September 20X3

Ref: YN/87/33

Dear Sirs

PAYMENT OF ACCOUNT: £2,340.20 [1]

I was sorry to learn of your complaint regarding a statement received from us indicating that payment of your account is overdue[2].

Having investigated the matter[3], I confirm that we did receive a cheque for £2,340.20[4] from you on the 26 August. I regret that this payment was incorrectly credited as a result of unforeseen pressures on our accounting procedures at that time[5]. I am pleased to report that the error has been rectified: your account is fully paid up and I have taken steps to ensure that its creditworthiness is not impaired by this incident[6].

Please accept my sincere apologies for the concern caused to you[7]. I do not anticipate any recurrence of this problem, but if I can be of any further assistance please do not hesitate to contact me directly[8].

Yours faithfully

R Coe

R Coe
Senior Accounts Clerk
Extension 3320

Note the following features in the above letter, which should be borne in mind whenever a business letter is sent.

Letter feature	Comments
[1] Letter title	Always be as clear as possible about the matter covered in the letter - a brief letter title is ideal.
[2] Tone	This letter is polite and appropriately apologetic, without being grovelling, defensive or impertinent.
[3] Action taken	Always state what action has been taken when investigating a customer complaint.
[4] Amounts and dates	Stating the exact amounts and the dates of disputed transactions is vital for the customer to understand what you are saying.

Letter feature	Comments
5 Cause of error	It is not strictly necessary to give an explanation for why something went wrong (in theory, the customer is simply concerned that it has been corrected) but it lets the customers see that you have control of the overall situation, even if mistakes are made occasionally.
6 Future action	Consider what effect an error might have on a customer in the future, and reassure them.
7 Apologise	It is polite and reassuring to the customer for you to apologise for the mistake, and to reassure them.
8 Further contact	Reassure the customer that any further queries on the matter will be readily dealt with; make sure your name, and preferably your extension number, are clear on the letter.

Example: Being chased for payment

You are Ms Mai Ling, Senior Accounts Clerk of Tradewell Office Products and Services Ltd, of Easy Street Manchester M12 7SL. It is 22 June.

Your firm has an account (No: 33521) with Britline Carriers plc, who transports many of your products for you. You have just received a statement from Britline, accompanied by the following letter.

BRITLINE CARRIERS PLC
Sutton Lane, Liverpool LW6 9BC
Telephone: 0151 – 324 7345/6

Directors: Registered office:
D Smith (Managing)   Sutton Lane Liverpool LW6 9BC
P Patel   Reg. No 34567
C Wilkes   Reg. in England

Ref: NC/nn TO 16   21 June 20X0

Accounts Department
Tradewell Office Products & Services Ltd
Easy St
MANCHESTER M12 7SL

Dear Sir

OVERDUE ACCOUNT: 33521

Further to the statement sent to you on 16 May 20X0 it appears that your account for April 20X0 totalling £1,402.70 remains outstanding. Please find enclosed a copy statement.

The terms of credit extended to your company were agreed as 30 days from receipt of statement.

We should appreciate settlement of the above account at your earliest convenience.

Yours faithfully

N Competant

N Competant
Accounts Department

enc

You check your files. A cheque for the outstanding amount was sent to Britline on 6 June, but no acknowledgement was received. You also wonder if you have forfeited your usual 5% prompt payment discount because of the error.

You need to write an appropriate letter of complaint and query.

TRADEWELL OFFICE PRODUCTS & SERVICES LTD
Easy Street, Manchester, M12 7SL

22 June 20X0

Our ref: ML/db
Your ref: NC/nn TO 16

Mr N Competant,
Accounts Department,
Britline Carriers plc.,
'Sutton Lane,
LIVERPOOL LW6 9BC

Dear Mr Competant,

ACCOUNT NUMBER 33521

I am concerned by the contents of your letter of 21 June, requesting payment of £1,402.70 outstanding on the above account for April 20X0.

Our files indicate that a cheque payment was made by us on 6 June, within 30 days of the statement dated 16 May. No acknowledgement of payment was received from you.

It would appear there has been an error of some kind, and I would be grateful if you would kindly consult your records.

I am also rather concerned that we may not have been credited with the usual 5% prompt payment discount in these circumstances. Perhaps you can reassure me on this point.

Yours sincerely,

Mai Ling

Mai Ling (Ms)
Senior Accounts Clerk

Notes

1   'Your ref' picks up the reference given on Britline's collection letter.

2   The tone is formal and 'civilised' throughout: the cheque may have been lost in the post - being abusive is of little value.

3   The letter starts by referring to Britline's communication, with relevant details. It then states the nature of your concern, and the actions you expect Britline to take.

Example: Dealing with a complaint

You are Mr M Barrast, Accounts Manager of Britline Carriers plc. TOPS' complaint has been referred to you and you discover that a cheque was indeed received from them on 7 June. Unfortunately, Britline lost two of its ledger clerks that week due to illness, and it appears that the temporary replacement credited £1,402.70 to another firm's account by mistake.

You need to write an appropriate letter of apology and explanation to Ms Ling at TOPS.

BRITLINE CARRIERS PLC

Sutton Lane, Liverpool LW6 9BC
Telephone: 0151 - 324 7345/6

Directors:
D Smith (Managing)
P Patel
C Wilkes

Registered office:
Sutton Lane
Liverpool LW6 9BC
Reg. No 34567
Reg. in England

Our ref: ML/nn TO 17
Your ref: ML/db

27 June 20X0

Ms M Ling
Senior Accounts Clerk
Tradewell Office Products & Services Ltd
Easy St
MANCHESTER M12 7SL

Dear Ms Ling

PAYMENT OF ACCOUNT: 33521

I was sorry to learn of your complaint of 22 June regarding the statement we sent you indicating that payment of your account was overdue.

Having checked our records, I discovered that we did indeed receive your cheque for £1,402.70 on 7 June. Due to unfortunate circumstances affecting our accounts department at that time, the payment was regrettably credited to another customer account. I am pleased to report that the error has been rectified and that your prompt payment discount has not been affected.

Please accept my sincere apologies for the concern caused to you in this matter. We anticipate no recurrence of our departmental problems, but if I can be of assistance in any other way, do not hesitate to contact me.

Yours sincerely

M Barrast

M Barrast
Accounts Manager

Notes

1   The reference picks up Ms Ling's last letter.

2   The tone is apologetic, but positive. Emphasis is on investigation and rectification of the mistake - not shame and guilt.

3   Again, the context is laid out first, followed by an explanation and summary. Note that the details of the clerk's illness etc were irrelevant.

4   Mr Barrast apologises for the 'concern' caused - not the 'inconvenience', which is an over-used cliché.

Activity 7.2

You are A Technician, Senior Accounts Assistant of Paywell Services Ltd of 24 Maidstone Road, Taunton TA4 4RP. The date is 24 February 20X7.

Your firm has an account number P942 with Recycle Ltd, a company with which you have traded for many months. Recycle Ltd offers a settlement discount of 2½% for payment within the credit terms. You have recently received a letter from Recycle as shown below.

 RECYCLE LIMITED

Jarvis Lane Maidenhead Berkshire SL6 4RS Tel: 01628 722722

Accounts Department
Paywell Services Ltd
24 Maidstone Road
Taunton TA4 4RP
Our ref: DW/SB 42

20 February 20X7

Dear Sir or Madam

OVERDUE ACCOUNT No. P942

I enclose a copy statement of account showing that £2,642.50 remains outstanding on your above account. The original statement was sent to you on 10 January 20X7, and the amount shown on this statement was payable within 30 days of the date of the statement.

We would appreciate immediate settlement of the above account.

Yours faithfully

D Waite

D Waite (Ms)
Accounts Department

On reviewing your files, you find that the outstanding balance was paid by BACS transfer (the usual method of payment to this creditor) on 31 January 20X7. In August and October 20X6, there had been correspondence between Paywell and Recycle Ltd due to Recycle's failure to credit BACS payments to the correct account.

Task

Write an appropriate letter to the creditor.

Answers to Activities

BPP
PROFESSIONAL EDUCATION

Answers to activities

Chapter 1

Answer 1.1

(a)

100,000	10,000	1,000	100	10	1
1	2	5	1	2	5
7	6	3	5	7	9
8	8	8	7	0	4
			+1	+1	

Answer: 888,704

(b)

1,000,000	100,000	10,000	1,000	100	10	1
1	7	6	0	2	2	0
5	1	2	0	7	6	3
6	8	8	0	9	8	3

Answer: 6,880,983

(c)

10,000,000	1,000,000	100,000	10,000	1,000	100	10	1
1	2	1	7	5	1	7	5
	4	3	2	1	0	0	0
1	6	4	9	6	1	7	5

Answer: 16,496,175

(d)

100,000,000	10,000,000	1,000,000	100,000	10,000	1,000	100	10	1
1	2	5	7	4	3	6	8	9
1	5	2	3	4	7	9	8	6
2	7	8	0	9	1	6	7	5
		+1		+1	+1	+1	+1	

Answer: 278,091,675

(e)

100,000	10,000	1,000	100	10	1
1	4	6	7	2	0
2	2	0	5	4	0
3	2	5	7	6	0
6	9	3	0	2	0
	+1	+2	+1		

Answer: 693,020

Answer 1.2

(a)

1,000,000	100,000	10,000	1,000	100	10	1
4	7	6	0	2	2	0
2	9	5	0	0	0	0
1	8	1	0	2	2	0
−1	+10					

Answer: 1,810,220

(b)

10,000,000	1,000,000	100,000	10,000	1,000	100	10	1
1	5	7	6	5	4	3	2
	4	5	6	0	7	8	9
1	1	2	0	4	6	4	3
				−1	+10 − 1	+10 − 1	+10

Answer: 11,204,643

(d)

100,000,000	10,000,000	1,000,000	100,000	10,000	1,000	100	10	1
1	2	5	1	2	5	1	2	5
	7	4	5	6	8	1	2	3
—	5	0	5	5	7	0	0	2
−1	+10	−1	+10 − 1	+10 − 1	+10			

Answer: 50,557,002

Answer 1.3

(a) Most of us know our 12 times table but if not you could multiply by 10, then multiply by 2 and add the two together.

10,000,000	1,000,000	100,000	10,000	1,000	100	10	1
	5	3	2	1	7	8	9
							12 ×
6	3	8	6	1	4	6	8
+6	+3	+2	+2	+9	+10	+10	

Answer: 63,861,468

or

10,000,000	1,000,000	100,000	10,000	1,000	100	10	1
	5	3	2	1	7	8	9
							2 ×
1	0	6	4	3	5	7	8
+1				+1	+1	+1	

$5,321,789 \times 10 = 53,217,890$

$53,217,890 + 10,643,578 = 63,861,468$

BPP PROFESSIONAL EDUCATION

(b)   1,476,572,000. Did you remember to just add '00' onto the end of the number?

(c)   1,476,572. When dividing by 10, just drop the final '0'.

(d)   As very few people are comfortable dividing by 50, the trick is to divide by 10 and then divide that answer by 5.

17,625,450 ÷ 10 = 1,762,545

1,000,000	100,000	10,000	1,000	100	10	1
1	7	6	2	5	4	5
						5 ÷
$\overline{0}$	$\overline{3}$	$\overline{5}$	$\overline{2}$	$\overline{5}$	$\overline{0}$	$\overline{9}$
	+10	+20	+10	+20		+40

Answer: 352,509

Answer 1.4

(a) $64 - (-1) = 64 + 1 = 65$

(b) $\dfrac{96}{12} + \dfrac{18}{-2} = 8 - 9 = -1$

(c) $8(-3) - (4 + 8) = -24 - 12 = -36$

(d) $\dfrac{-36}{6} - \dfrac{84}{-7} + \dfrac{81}{3} = -6 + 12 + 27 = 33$

Answer 1.5

(a) $x = (3y - 20)^2$

Take the square root of each side.

$\sqrt{x} = 3y - 20$

Add 20 to each side

$\sqrt{x} + 20 = 3y$

Divide each side by 3 and swop sides for ease of reading

$y = \dfrac{\sqrt{x} + 20}{3}$

(b) $2(y - 4) - 4(x^2 + 3) = 0$

So:

$4(x^2 + 3) = 2 (y - 4)$

Divide each side by 4

$$x^2 + 3 = \frac{2(y-4)}{4}$$

Subtract 3 from each side

$$x^2 = \frac{2(y-4)}{4} - 3$$

$$x^2 = \frac{2y}{4} - \frac{8}{4} - 3$$

$$x^2 = \frac{y}{2} - 5$$

Take square root of each side

$$x = \sqrt{\frac{y}{2} - 5}$$

Answer 1.6

5x+2y = 34	(1)
x + 3y = 25	(2)

Multiply (2) × 5

5x + 15y = 125	(3)

Deduct (1) from (3)

$$5x + 15y - 5x - 2y = 125 - 34$$
$$13y = 91$$
$$y = 7$$

Put this value into (2)

$$x + 21 = 25$$
$$x = 25 - 21$$
$$x = 4$$

Answer: x = 4, y = y

BPP
PROFESSIONAL EDUCATION

Chapter 2

Answer 2.1

The discount is 17% × £395 = $\frac{17}{100}$ × 395

= £67.15

Discounted price is therefore £327.85   (£395 – £67.15)

Alternatively, you could say that the brochure price is 100% and the discount is 17%. Therefore the discounted price is 83% (100% – 17%).

83% × £395 = £327.85

Answer 2.2

The key wording is the mark-up of 20% is **on cost**. This means that cost is 100%, mark-up is 20% and so the selling price is 120%.

Therefore original cost = $\frac{200}{120}$ × 100 = £166.67

Check:

	£
Original cost (100%)	166.67
Mark-up (20%)	33.33
Selling price (120%)	200.00

Answer 2.3

Selling price	100%
Cost	95%
Gross profit	5%

Gross profit is 5% of sales.

So, in this case, cost   = $\frac{95}{100}$ × £200

= £190

Answer 2.4

(a) **Tutorial note**. Just because there are four people rather than two does not mean that the question is more difficult. Calculate the total number of parts. Calculate the value of one part. Then allocate the correct number of parts to each person.

Total number of parts: 6 + 1 + 2 + 3 = 12
Value of one part = £600 ÷ 12 = £50

	£
A = 6 parts = 6 × £50	300
B = 1 part = 1 × £50	50
C = 2 parts = 2 × £50	100
D = 3 parts = 3 × £50	150
	600

(b) Number of parts = 5 + 3 + 2 = 10

One part = $\frac{£1,000}{10}$ = £100

	£
A = 5 parts	500
B = 3 parts	300
C = 2 parts	200
	1,000

(c) Number of parts = 4 + 3 + 3 = 10

One part = $\frac{£100}{10}$ = £10

	£
Bob = 4 parts	40
Charlie = 3 parts	30
Dave = 3 parts	30
	100

(d) Number of parts = 2 + 2 + 1 + 1 = 6

One part = $\frac{£12,000}{6}$ = £2,000

BPP
PROFESSIONAL EDUCATION

	£
A = 2 parts	4,000
B = 2 parts	4,000
C = 1 part	2,000
D = 1 part	2,000
	12,000

Answer 2.5

(a)   4 (4 × 4 = 16)

(b)   30

(c)   55

(d)   121

Chapter 3

Answer 3.1

(a) Extremely unlikely. If Biff got these wages every week his or her annual salary would £56,662.84. Even if Biff earned a huge amount of overtime this week, this seems a very high rate of pay for the job. The only possible explanation is that Biff has received a large amount of back pay and/or a very large bonus this week. It seems most likely, though, that a mistake has been made somewhere.

(b) Yes. £25,000 ÷ 4 = £6,250, so the salary to date of £6,211.67 is reasonable.

(c) No. Her basic salary this month is £1,500 (£18,000 ÷ 12). Her overtime should be £450 (30 hours at £15 per hour). The gross pay total should be £1,950. It looks as if the overtime was calculated as 3 hours, not 30 hours.

Answer 3.2

(a)

(i)	£1	£482,365
(ii)	£100	£482,400
(iii)	£1,000	£482,000
(iv)	£10,000	£480,000

(b)

(i)	843.7
(ii)	843.67

Answer 3.3

The maximum absolute error = 50p = £0.50 because £9.50 would be rounded up to £10.00 but £9.49 would be rounded down to £9.00.

$$\text{The maximum relative error} = \frac{\text{maximum absolute error}}{\text{estimate}} \times 100\%$$

$$= \frac{£0.50}{£10.00} \times 100\% = 5\%$$

The correct answer is B.

Chapter 4

Answer 4.1

Probability

Ace	Spade	Ace of spades	Ace or spade
4/52	13/52	1/52	4/3

Working

P(ace or spade) = 4/52 + 13/52 − 1/52 = 16/52 = 4/13

Answer 4.2

(a) The probability of at least one computer error is 1 minus the probability of no error. The probability of no error is $0.9 \times 0.8 \times 0.7 = 0.504$.

(Since the probability of an error is 0.1, 0.2 and 0.3 in each section, the probability of no error in each section must be 0.9, 0.8 and 0.7 respectively.)

The probability of at least one error is 1 − 0.504 = 0.496.

(b) Y = yes, N = no

		Section 1	Section 2	Section 3
(i)	Error?	Y	N	N
(ii)	Error?	N	Y	N
(iii)	Error?	N	N	Y

		Probabilities
(i)	$0.1 \times 0.8 \times 0.7$ =	0.056
(ii)	$0.9 \times 0.2 \times 0.7$ =	0.126
(iii)	$0.9 \times 0.8 \times 0.3$ =	0.216
	Total	0.398

The probability of only one error only is 0.398.

Answer 4.3

P(male) = 60% = 0.6

P(female) = 1 − 0.6 = 0.4

P(CIMA candidate) = 75% = 0.75

We need to use the general rule of addition to avoid double counting.

∴ P(female or CIMA candidate) = P(female) + P(CIMA candidate) − P(female *and* CIMA candidate)

$$= 0.4 + 0.75 - (0.4 \times 0.75)$$
$$= 1.15 - 0.3$$
$$= 0.85$$

The correct answer is A.

You should have been able to eliminate options C and D immediately. 0.4 is the probability that the candidate is female and 1.00 is the probability that something will definitely happen - neither of these options are likely to correspond to the probability that the candidate is both female or a CIMA candidate.

Answer 4.4

One standard deviation corresponds to z = 1

If z = 1, we can look this value up in normal distribution tables to get a value (area) of 0.3413. One standard deviation above the mean can be shown on a graph as follows.

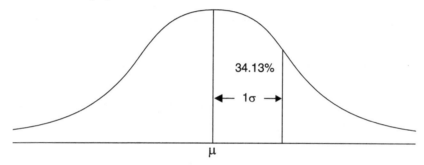

The normal distribution is symmetrical, and we must therefore show the area corresponding to one standard deviation below the mean on the graph also.

①   The area one standard deviation *below* the mean

②   The area one standard deviation *above* the mean

Area one standard deviation above *and* below the mean

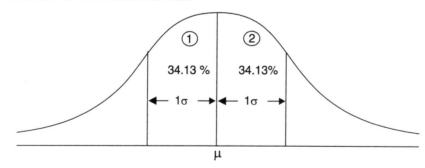

$$= \;\; ① \;\; + \;\; ②$$
$$= \;\; 34.13\% + 34.13\%$$
$$= \;\; 68.26\% ≃ 68\%$$

Answer 4.5

(a)

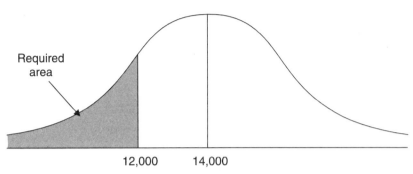

$$z \;\; = \;\; \frac{12,000 - 14,000}{2,700}$$

$$= \;\; -0.74$$

From normal distribution tables, the proportion of salaries between £12,000 and £14,000 is 0.2704 (from tables). The proportion of salaries less than £12,000 is therefore 0.5 − 0.2704 = 0.2296.

(b)

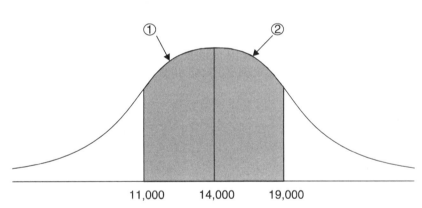

① $\quad z \;\; = \;\; \dfrac{11,000 - 14,000}{2,700}$

$\qquad\quad = \;\; 1.11$

② $\quad z \;\; = \;\; \dfrac{19,000 - 14,000}{2,700}$

$\qquad\quad = \;\; 1.85$

The proportion with earnings between £11,000 and £14,000 is 0.3665 (from tables where z = 1.11).

The proportion with earnings between £14,000 and £19,000 is 0.4678 (from tables where z = 1.85).

The required proportion is therefore 0.3665 + 0.4678 = 0.8343.

Answer 4.6

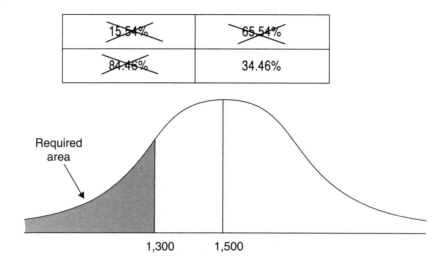

$$z = \frac{x - \mu}{\sigma}$$

$$= \frac{1,300 - 1,500}{500}$$

$$= 0.4$$

A z score of 0.4 corresponds to a probability of 0.1554 (ie probability that sales are between 1,300 and 1,500). The probability that sales are less than 1,300 = 0.5 − 0.1554 = 0.3446 or 34.46%.

Answer 4.7

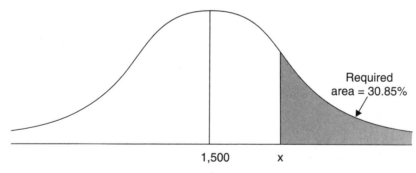

The probability that sales are between 1,500 and x items per week is found as follows. The shaded area = 30.85% (probability sales are greater than x). The probability that sales are between 1,500 and x = 50% - 30.85% = 19.15% = 0.1915. 0.1915 corresponds to a z score of 0.5.

$$\therefore \quad z = \frac{x - \mu}{\sigma}$$

$$\therefore \quad 0.5 = \frac{x - 1,500}{500}$$

$$\therefore \quad x = (0.5 \times 500) + 1,500$$

$$= 1,750 \text{ items}$$

The correct answer is therefore C.

Answer 4.8

Value now	Investment period	Interest rate	Final value
£	Years	%	£
5,000	3	20	8,640.00 [1]
5,000	4	15	8,745.03 [2]
5,000	3	6	5,955.08 [3]

Workings

(1) $£5,000 \times 1.20^3 = £8,640.00$

(2) $£5,000 \times 1.15^4 = £8,745.03$

(3) $£5,000 \times 1.06^3 = £5,955.08$

Answer 4.9

Using the formula for compound interest, $S = X(1 + r)^n$, we know that X = £2,000, S = £2,721 and n = 4. We need to find r. It is essential that you are able to rearrange equations confidently when faced with this type of multiple choice question - there is not a lot of room for guessing!

$$2,721 = 2,000 \times (1 + r)^4$$
$$(1 + r)^4 = 2,721/2,000 = 1.3605$$
$$1 + r = \sqrt[4]{1.3605} = 1.08$$
$$r = 0.08 = 8\%$$

The correct answer is B.

Answer 4.10

£7,104

Working

Using the discounting formula, $X = S \times \dfrac{1}{(1+r)^n}$

where   S = £16,000
n = 12
r = 0.07
X = PV

$PV = £16,000 \times \dfrac{1}{1.07^{12}} = £7,104$

Chapter 5

Answer 5.1

(a) Cells into which you would need to enter a value are: B4, B5, B6, C4, C5, C6, D4, D5 and D6. Cells which would perform calculations are B7, C7, D7, E4, E5, E6 and E7.

(b) (i) =B4+B5+B6 *or better* =SUM(B4:B6)

(ii) =B6+C6+D6 *or better* =SUM(B6:D6)

(iii) =E4+E5+E6 *or better* =SUM(E4:E6) Alternatively, the three monthly totals could be added across the spreadsheet: = SUM (B7: D7)

(c) The figures which would change, besides the amount in cell C5, would be those in cells C7, E5 and E7. (The contents of E7 would change if *any* of the sales figures changed.)

Chapter 7

Answer 7.1

FELLOWS PLC

MEMORANDUM

To: Ashram Khan
From: Chan Yuan, Payroll Clerk
Date: 01/05/X4
Subject: Increase in Peter Piper's salary

Thank you for your memo of 30 April.

However Peter Piper's salary is currently £30,000 pa. Therefore I cannot implement your instructions. Please can you let me have revised instructions.

ChanYuan

Notes

1   The first sentence refers to Ashram Kahn's previous memo, so both parties know what this memo is about.

2   The second sentence states Peter Piper's current salary.

3   The third sentence details the problem (that the chairman's instructions cannot be followed).

4   The fourth sentence asks for revised instructions.

Although your memo may be worded differently, it should contain the same general information: the memo being questioned, the problem and asking for revised instructions or clarification.

Answer 7.2

PAYWELL SERVICES LIMITED
24 Maidstone Road, Taunton TA4 4RP

Ms D Waite
Accounts Department
Recycle Limited
Jarvis Lane
Maidenhead
SL6 4RS

Your ref: DW/SB 42

24 February 20X7

Dear Ms Waite,

Account number - P942

I am concerned at having received your letter of 20 February 20X7 stating that £2,642.50 remains outstanding on the above account for December 20X6.

Our records show that payment of this amount was made by BACS under the usual reference on 31 January. We have not received any acknowledgement of the payment from you.

It would seem that some error has been made, and I would be grateful if you would check whether you have a record of the payment. I note that on previous occasions there have been some problems in matching BACS payments to our account.

I am also concerned that we may not have been credited with the usual 2½% discount for prompt payment. Can you reassure me on this point?

Yours faithfully

A Technician

Senior Accounts Assistant

Glossary of accounting terms

There is a range of **documentation** that you may encounter in your studies and if you work in a financial environment. Some of the more common ones are listed with an explanation of their function

Advice Note	This is a document sent by the supplier of goods to the buyer to advise that the goods are being despatched.
Bank Statement	At regular intervals and in the case of a large organisation, daily, this document shows the bank balance on the organisation's account as seen by the bank. It rarely agrees with the organisation's own records therefore an exercise to reconcile the two balances may need to be performed to allow for timing differences.
Cheque	One of the most common methods of settling debts, this is a mandate allowing the debtor (who is owed money) to claim it from the creditor (who owes the money) by paying a cheque into a bank account, so that settlement of the debt can be completed by the banks own clearing system.
Consignment Note	When a third party haulier, not the seller, is making the delivery of the goods, a consignment note goes with the goods. The haulier has responsibility for the goods during transit. A representative of the buyer, often the storekeeper, normally signs a copy to confirm delivery and this is returned to the seller as proof of delivery.
Credit Note	A credit note is used to correct an invoice that may be wrong for a variety of reasons eg part delivery, overcharge, faulty or inappropriate goods.
Debit Note	This is sent by the buyer to request a credit note when the original invoice proves to be incorrect.
Delivery Note	This works in exactly the same way as the consignment note but is used when the seller is also making the delivery.
Enquiry	This is a request for information about the range of products, services and prices sent by a potential new customer before any firm orders are placed. It does not represent any agreement to enter into a contract between the parties; it is a request for information only.
Invoice	Sent by the seller it is a request for a debt to be settled at the appropriate time as agreed.
Order	If an enquiry has been successful an order will be placed which has contractual status.
Order Processing	Where a large order has been placed or the order could take some time to complete the buyer may send an order processing form to check on the status of the work and to confirm that delivery is still on schedule.

Statement

This works in a similar way to a bank statement but is sent by the debtor (who is owed money) to the creditor (who owes the money) showing the current state of the account. It is normally sent monthly showing the opening balance at the beginning of the month, transactions during the month and the closing balance at the month end.

Stock/Stores
Record Card

This is a manual system used by Stores showing which goods are available and in what quantities. It will also show the point at which more need to be ordered and the quantity of the re-order.

The following are supporting books and are not normally part of the double entry process, the exception being the Cash Book. They are often referred to as **books of prime or original entry** because they are the first point of entry of a document.

Cash Book

Where the cash and bank accounts are maintained in the Main Ledger the Cash Book itself will be a memorandum record only and used to record flows of money into and out of the organisation. However it is worth remembering that the Cash Book can also be a Ledger.

Journal

This book has three main functions. It can be used as a book of prime entry when others are not suitable for use to open new accounts. It can also be used to record unusual entries. This is more likely during the early life of an organisation. Once the organisation develops it is more likely to be used to make corrections or amendments to existing entries.

Instead of being used as some form of continuous book, vouchers may be used to initiate journal entries especially when there is much repetition of type of entry.

Purchase Daybook

Sometimes called the Purchase Journal, it is used to record all invoices received. Therefore it is an invoice listing. Where an organisation buys a range of goods the daybook may be analysed into categories of goods. In a computerised system the invoice listing fulfils the same function.

Purchase Returns Daybook

Sometimes called the Returns Outward Journal or Daybook it is used to record all credit notes received. Therefore it is a credit note listing. If the Purchase Daybook is analysed then so too will be the Returns Book. In a computerised system the credit note listing fulfils the same function.

Sales Daybook

Sometimes called the Sales Journal, this is used to record all invoices sent out. Therefore it is an invoice listing .Where an organisation sells a range of goods the daybook may be analysed into categories of goods. In a computerised system the invoice listing fulfil the same function.

Sales Returns Daybook

Sometimes called the Returns Inward Journal or Daybook, this is used to record all credit notes sent out. Therefore it is a credit note listing. If the Sales Daybook is analysed then so too will be the Returns Book. In a computerised system the credit note listing fulfils the same function.

Petty Cash Book

When an organisation deals primarily with cheques the main Cash Book will be used for them and a Petty Cash Book will be established to record and analyse those cash transactions that it perceives to be of petty (small) amounts.

BPP PROFESSIONAL EDUCATION

The following records are those that can be part of the **double entry process** and thus provide the data needed to construct the Trial Balance and the final accounts of an organisation.

Cash Book

Used to record movements of money into and out of the business. There are many different ways of displaying this data from the one, two, three or four column presentation to those that contain records of cheques received and sent out only, cash transactions being recorded elsewhere.

Sometimes the Cash Book is a memorandum record only, (not part of the double entry system), cash and bank accounts being shown as part of the double entry process in the Main Ledger.

It is important when learning about the Cash Book to understand how it works and then to be familiar with different styles and layouts prior to testing.

Main Ledger

This has been known variously as the General Ledger and Nominal Ledger but AAT has indicated that it will be using the term Main Ledger in the future.

The Main Ledger contains three types of accounts. It contains all personal/private accounts eg drawings or capital. It also contains real accounts ie assets such as buildings, office equipment, etc., owned by the business. Finally the impersonal accounts themselves are included ie expenses such as rent, wages, control accounts etc.

In a computerised system the coding will usually reflect where the account balance will be found in the month end or year end accounts.

Purchase Ledger

Sometimes called the Bought Ledger this is a listing of creditors ie those to whom we owe money. It may be subdivided alphabetically, by region, buyer or type of creditor.

The Purchase Ledger may be part of the double entry system by taking the total of the balances from individual accounts and using that total in the Trial Balance for creditors.

It is more common today to use the Purchase Ledger as a memorandum record and refer to it as a Subsidiary Ledger. Total creditors would be obtained from a control account found in the Main Ledger.

Sales Ledger

This is a listing of debtors and can be subdivided in a similar way to the Purchase Ledger.

It is more common today to obtain the debtors total from a control account in the Main Ledger than to maintain the Sales Ledger as part of the double entry system. In this case the Sales Ledger would be referred to as a Subsidiary Ledger.

The following list gives a comparison of UK and International accounting terms.

UK	International
Books of prime entry	Books of original entry
Creditors	Payables
Creditors due within one year	Current liabilities
Creditors due over one year	Non current liabilities, or long term liabilities
Debtors	Receivables
Depreciation provision (balance sheet)	Accumulated depreciation
Fixed assets	Non current assets
Intercompany trading	Intra-group trading
Limited company	Limited liability company
Plc	Inc
Preference shares/preference dividend	Preferred shares/preferred dividends
Profit and loss account	Income statement
Provision for doubtful debts	Allowance for doubtful debts
Retained profit (or profit and loss reserves)	Revenue reserves
Statement of total recognised gains and losses	Statement of recognised gains and losses
Stock	Inventory

See overleaf for information on other
BPP products and how to order

CIMA Order

To BPP Professional Education, Aldine Place, London W12 8AW

Tel: 020 8740 2211 — Fax: 020 8740 1184
email: publishing@bpp.com — website: www.bpp.com
Order online www.bpp.com

Occasionally we may wish to email you relevant offers and information about courses and products. Please tick to opt into this service. ☐

Mr/Mrs/Ms (Full name)

Daytime delivery address

Postcode

Daytime Tel

Email

Date of exam (month/year)

POSTAGE & PACKING

Study Texts and Kits

	First	Each extra	Online
UK	£5.00	£2.00	£2.00
Europe*	£6.00	£4.00	£4.00
Rest of world	£20.00	£10.00	£10.00

Passcards/Success Tapes/MCQ Cards/CDs/Posters

	First	Each extra	Online
UK	£2.00	£1.00	£1.00
Europe*	£3.00	£2.00	£2.00
Rest of world	£8.00	£8.00	£8.00

Grand Total (incl. Postage) £

I enclose a cheque for
(Cheques to BPP Professional Education)

Or charge to Visa/Mastercard/Switch

Card Number

Expiry date — Start Date

Issue Number (Switch Only)

Signature

CERTIFICATE / FOUNDATION*	5/04 Texts	1/04 Kits	1/04 Passcards	Big Picture Posters	Success CDs	Virtual Campus	8/04 i-Pass	10/04 i-Learn	11/04 MCQ cards
C1 Management Accounting Fundamentals (Foundation 2)	£24.95 ☐	£10.95 ☐	£6.95 ☐	£6.95 ☐	£14.95 ☐	£50 ☐	£24.95 ☐		
C2 Financial Accounting Fundamentals (Foundation 1)	£24.95 ☐	£10.95 ☐	£6.95 ☐	£6.95 ☐	£14.95 ☐	£50 ☐	£24.95 ☐		
C3 Business Mathematics (Foundation 3c)	£24.95 ☐	£10.95 ☐	£6.95 ☐	£6.95 ☐	£14.95 ☐	£50 ☐	£24.95 ☐		
C4 Economics for Business (Foundation 3a)	£24.95 ☐	£10.95 ☐	£6.95 ☐	£6.95 ☐	£14.95 ☐	£50 ☐	£24.95 ☐		
C5 Business Law (Foundation 3b)	£24.95 ☐	£10.95 ☐	£6.95 ☐	£6.95 ☐	£14.95 ☐	£50 ☐	£24.95 ☐		
MANAGERIAL	**7/04 Texts**	**1/05 Kits**	**1/05 Passcards**				**9/04 i-Pass**		
P1 Management Accounting - Performance Evaluation	£24.95 ☐	£12.95 ☐	£9.95 ☐	£6.95 ☐	£14.95 ☐	£90 ☐	£24.95 ☐	£34.95 ☐	£9.95 ☐
P2 Management Accounting - Decision Management	£24.95 ☐	£12.95 ☐	£9.95 ☐	£6.95 ☐	£14.95 ☐	£90 ☐	£24.95 ☐	£34.95 ☐	£9.95 ☐
P4 Organisational Management and Information Systems	£24.95 ☐	£12.95 ☐	£9.95 ☐	£6.95 ☐	£14.95 ☐	£90 ☐	£24.95 ☐	£34.95 ☐	£9.95 ☐
P5 Integrated Management	£24.95 ☐	£12.95 ☐	£9.95 ☐	£6.95 ☐	£14.95 ☐	£90 ☐	£24.95 ☐	£34.95 ☐	£9.95 ☐
P7 Financial Accounting and Tax Principles	£24.95 ☐	£12.95 ☐	£9.95 ☐	£6.95 ☐	£14.95 ☐	£90 ☐	£24.95 ☐	£34.95 ☐	£9.95 ☐
P8 Financial Analysis	£24.95 ☐	£12.95 ☐	£9.95 ☐	£6.95 ☐	£14.95 ☐	£90 ☐	£24.95 ☐	£34.95 ☐	£9.95 ☐
STRATEGIC									
P3 Management Accounting - Risk and Control Strategy	£24.95 ☐	£12.95 ☐	£9.95 ☐	£6.95 ☐	£14.95 ☐				
P6 Management Accounting - Business Strategy	£24.95 ☐	£12.95 ☐	£9.95 ☐	£6.95 ☐	£14.95 ☐				
P9 Management Accounting - Financial Strategy	£24.95 ☐	£12.95 ☐	£9.95 ☐	£6.95 ☐	£14.95 ☐				
P10 Test of Professional Competence in Management Accounting (TOPCIMA)		£24.95 ☐ (For 5/05: available 3/05)			£14.95 ☐				

Toolkit — £24.95 ☐

Learning to Learn Accountancy (7/02) — £9.95 ☐

Total ☐

*For material published before May 2004, Certificate assessments were known as Foundation assessments and numbered as shown. The syllabuses for these assessments are unchanged.

We aim to deliver to all UK addresses inside 5 working days. A signature will be required. Orders to all EU addresses should be delivered within 6 working days. All other orders to overseas addresses should be delivered within 8 working days. *Europe includes the Republic of Ireland and the Channel Islands.

See overleaf for information on other
BPP products and how to order

ACCA Order

To BPP Professional Education, Aldine Place, London W12 8AW

Tel: 020 8740 2211
email: publishing@bpp.com
Order online www.bpp.com
Fax: 020 8740 1184
website: www.bpp.com

Mr/Mrs/Ms (Full name) _____

Daytime delivery address _____

Postcode _____

Daytime Tel _____

Date of exam (month/year) _____   Scots law variant   Y / N

Occasionally we may wish to email you relevant offers and information about courses and products. Please tick to opt into this service. ☐

	6/04 Texts	1/04 Kits	1/04 Passcards	***Success CDs	Big Picture Posters	8/04 i-Learn	8/04 i-Pass	Virtual Campus
PART 1								
1.1 Preparing Financial Statements	£24.95	£10.95	£6.95	£14.95	£6.95	£34.95	£24.95	£90
1.2 Financial Information for Management	£24.95	£10.95	£6.95	£14.95	£6.95	£34.95	£24.95	£90
1.3 Managing People	£24.95	£10.95	£6.95	£14.95	£6.95	£34.95	£24.95	£90
PART 2								
2.1 Information Systems	£24.95	£10.95	£6.95	£14.95	£6.95	£34.95	£24.95	£90
2.2 Corporate and Business Law **	£24.95	£10.95	£6.95	£14.95	£6.95	£34.95	£24.95	£90
2.3 Business Taxation FA2003 (12/04 exams)	£20.95	£10.95	£6.95	£14.95	£6.95	£34.95	£24.95	£90
2.3 Business Taxation FA2004 (8/04 for 6/05 exams)†	£24.95							
2.4 Financial Management and Control	£24.95	£10.95	£6.95	£14.95	£6.95	£34.95	£24.95	£90
2.5 Financial Reporting	£24.95	£10.95	£6.95	£14.95	£6.95	£34.95	£24.95	£90
2.6 Audit and Internal Review (12/04 exams)	£24.95	£10.95	£6.95	£14.95	£6.95	£34.95	£24.95	£90
2.6 Audit and Internal Review (9/04 for 6/05 exams)†	£24.95							
PART 3								
3.1 Audit and Assurance Services	£24.95	£10.95	£6.95	£14.95	£6.95	£34.95	£24.95	£90
3.2 Advanced Taxation FA2003 (12/04 exams)	£20.95	£10.95	£6.95	£14.95	£6.95	£34.95	£24.95	£90
3.2 Advanced Taxation FA2004 (9/04 for 6/05 exams)†	£24.95							
3.3 Performance Management	£24.95	£10.95	£6.95	£14.95	£6.95	£34.95	£24.95	£90
3.4 Business Information Management	£24.95	£10.95	£6.95	£14.95	£6.95	£34.95	£24.95	£90
3.5 Strategic Business Planning and Development	£24.95	£10.95	£6.95	£14.95	£6.95	£34.95	£24.95	£90
3.6 Advanced Corporate Reporting	£24.95	£10.95	£6.95	£14.95	£6.95	£34.95	£24.95	£90
3.7 Strategic Financial Management	£24.95	£10.95	£6.95	£14.95	£6.95	£34.95	£24.95	£90
INTERNATIONAL STREAM								
1.1 Preparing Financial Statements	£24.95	£10.95	£6.95			£34.95	£24.95	
2.2 Corporate and Business Law	£24.95	£10.95	£6.95					
2.5 Financial Reporting	£24.95	£10.95	£6.95			£34.95	£24.95	
2.6 Audit and Internal Review	£24.95	£10.95	£6.95			£34.95	£24.95	
3.1 Audit and Assurance Services	£24.95	£10.95	£6.95				£24.95	
3.6 Advanced Corporate Reporting	£24.95	£10.95	£6.95				£24.95	
Success in Your Research and Analysis								
Project - Tutorial Text (10/04)	£24.95							
Learning to Learn (7/02)	£9.95							

SUBTOTAL £ _____

POSTAGE & PACKING

Study Texts

	First	Each extra	Online	
UK	£5.00	£2.00	£2.00	£
Europe*	£6.00	£4.00	£4.00	£
Rest of world	£20.00	£10.00	£10.00	£

Kits

	First	Each extra	Online	
UK	£5.00	£2.00	£2.00	£
Europe*	£6.00	£4.00	£4.00	£
Rest of world	£20.00	£10.00	£10.00	£

Passcards/Success Tapes/CDs

	First	Each extra	Online	
UK	£2.00	£1.00	£1.00	£
Europe*	£3.00	£2.00	£2.00	£
Rest of world	£8.00	£8.00	£8.00	£

Grand Total (incl. Postage)   £ _____

I enclose a cheque for _____
(Cheques to *BPP Professional Education*)

Or charge to Visa/Mastercard/Switch

Card Number _____

Expiry date _____   Start Date _____

Issue Number (Switch Only) _____

Signature _____

We aim to deliver to all UK addresses inside 5 working days; a signature will be required. Orders to all EU addresses should be delivered within 6 working days. All other orders to overseas addresses should be delivered within 8 working days. * Europe includes the Republic of Ireland and the Channel Islands. † For 6/05 exam, **New edition Kit, Passcard, i-Learn and i-Pass available 2005** . ** For Scots law variant students, a free **Scots Law Supplement** is available with the 2.2 Text. Please indicate in the name and address section if this applies to you. ***Alternatively, Success Tapes are available for the same papers, all £12.95.

Review Form & Free Prize Draw – Business Maths and English (6/04)

All original review forms from the entire BPP range, completed with genuine comments, will be entered into one of two draws on 31 January 2005 and 31 July 2005. The names on the first four forms picked out on each occasion will be sent a cheque for £50.

Name: _____   Address: _____

_____

_____

How have you used this Workbook?
(Tick one box only)

☐ Home study (book only)

☐ On a course: college _____

☐ With 'correspondence' package

☐ Other _____

Why did you decide to purchase this Workbook? *(Tick one box only)*

☐ Have used BPP Texts in the past

☐ Recommendation by friend/colleague

☐ Recommendation by a lecturer at college

☐ Saw advertising

☐ Other _____

During the past six months do you recall seeing/receiving any of the following?
(Tick as many boxes as are relevant)

☐ Our advertisement in *CIMA Insider / Financial Management*

☐ Our advertisement in *ACCA Student Accountant*

☐ Our brochure with a letter through the post

Which (if any) aspects of our advertising do you find useful?
(Tick as many boxes as are relevant)

☐ Prices and publication dates of new editions

☐ Information on Workbook content

☐ Facility to order books off-the-page

☐ None of the above

Your ratings, comments and suggestions would be appreciated on the following areas

	Very useful	Useful	Not useful
Introduction	☐	☐	☐
Chapter contents lists	☐	☐	☐
Examples	☐	☐	☐
Activities and answers	☐	☐	☐

	Excellent	Good	Adequate	Poor
Overall opinion of this Text	☐	☐	☐	☐

Do you intend to continue using BPP Interactive Texts/Assessment Kits?   ☐ Yes   ☐ No

Please note any further comments and suggestions/errors on the reverse of this page.

The BPP author of this edition can be e-mailed at: janiceross@bpp.com

Please return this form to: Janice Ross, BPP Professional Education, FREEPOST, London, W12 8BR

Review Form & Free Prize Draw (continued)

Please note any further comments and suggestions/errors below

Free Prize Draw Rules

1   Closing date for 31 January 2005 draw is 31 December 2004. Closing date for 31 July 2005 draw is 30 June 2005.

2   Restricted to entries with UK and Eire addresses only. BPP employees, their families and business associates are excluded.

3   No purchase necessary. Entry forms are available upon request from BPP Professional Education. No more than one entry per title, per person. Draw restricted to persons aged 16 and over.

4   Winners will be notified by post and receive their cheques not later than 6 weeks after the relevant draw date.

5   The decision of the promoter in all matters is final and binding. No correspondence will be entered into.